THE UNWAVERING EYE
SELECTED POEMS 1969-1975

THE UNWAVERING EYE

Selected Poems 1969~1975

BY
IRVING LAYTON
With a foreword by Eli Mandel

McClelland and Stewart Limited

ISBN: 7710-4844-0

The Canadian Publishers
McClelland and Stewart
25 Hollinger Road, Toronto

Printed and bound in Canada by
T. H. Best Printing Company Limited

For Wynne Francis

CONTENTS
Foreword by Eli Mandel

LOVERS AND LESSER MEN

SEVENTY-FIVE GREEK POEMS 1951-1974

FOREWORD

In the late sixties the need for a selected volume of Irving Layton's poetry became fully apparent. Earlier retrospective selections (such as *The Improved Binoculars* and *A Red Carpet For The Sun*), were out of print. A very large and significant body of poetry (some seventeen books published from 1945 to 1968), needed to be brought into sharp focus so that the main lines of Layton's concerns and the nature of his achievement could be discerned, not only by that increasingly large number of readers anxious to understand a controversial and exciting writer, but by students and critics disconcerted by his technical virtuosity, and distracted by misleading arguments and quarrels about his character, his poetics, and his career. Wynne Francis's *Selected Poems* in 1969 sought to answer to these needs, "to focus attention," as she puts it in her Preface, "on some of the more enduring of Layton's poems."

Now, some six years later, the need for another selection is obvious. What had been made clear by 1968 not only needs to be said, but re-said as well. For from 1968 to the present, far from receding into the depths of his selections or remaining content with the massive assertions of *The Collected Poems of Irving Layton* (1971), Layton has continued to publish, with each new volume displaying the deepening nature of his vision, and the consolidation of his technical mastery in a variety of forms. It is to highlight that development in his writing and vision that the present volume, *The Unwavering Eye: Selected Poems 1969-1975,* appears and is placed alongside a soon to be published new edition of the earlier *Selected Poems: 1945-1968.* It presents the best poems of five volumes published since 1968 and marks out the newest, perhaps the most challenging, certainly the most accomplished articulation of Layton's critique of contemporary culture and civilization.

As in his earlier volumes, his style and form, various and capacious, depend for their success on what he himself has called the "imperial rhetoric" of poetry, a vivid, fluent line and passionate language that scorn the levelling "republican diction" of younger writers. In that opposition of the imperial and the republican, we can recognize the younger Layton's aligning of himself with the prophetic and visionary traditions of poetry. But now, that imperial voice lends itself not only to his early themes of celebration of desire, condemnation of evil, the tension between flux and form, but more particularly to a recognition of the historical and symbolic significance of the Jewish experience for our understanding of contemporary society and its values.

He is still ready at a moment's notice to sharpen an epigram on the edge of his hatred of philistines, to drag respectability out of the door with a few well-chosen quatrains of bawdy verse, to praise a whore or a beautiful woman, or for that matter, an ugly one, in sensuous loving lines. But alongside the celebrations of an aging and vital lover, something more disturbing moves through these later poems. Sometimes he speaks of this as the Jewish experience, and at other times as the enormous cruelty of modern man, his capacity for savagery, his "gentility." Layton has written:

> Today the disparity between rhetoric and experience
> has taken a form different from that of the forties,
> one which I find more sinister than the earlier one.
> It is also, I believe, at the root of the continuing
> gentility which afflicted this country for the better
> part of a century, if not since its very beginnings.
> I indicated in the prefaces I wrote for *Balls for a*
> *One-Armed Juggler* and *The Shattered Plinths* that the
> poetic rhetoric of our times has not attempted to
> assimilate the experience of Auschwitz, Belsen, and
> Gulag. This is true for the poets living in English-
> speaking countries, not true for poets in Poland,
> Czechoslovakia, and Germany. I am, I think, the only
> poet in any English-speaking country to have pointed
> this out. But this gentility is only part of a
> larger gentility that averts its courteous gaze from
> the cruelties and harrowing injustices Western
> Christendom has visited on Jews and still continues
> to do so. This gentility, it should be said, has
> consequences equally important and damaging both for
> Jew and gentile.

Challenging words. But then the younger Layton never promised us he would in an older year mellow. Darker now, often angrier, even misanthropic, he rages like an old prophet, and like an old prophet he strikes fire out of rock and calls together in those sparks visions of past, present, and future that we may know ourselves anew, as if for the first time.

Eli Mandel

October, 1974

THE UNWAVERING EYE
SELECTED POEMS 1969-1975

from *The Whole Bloody Bird*

THE SKULL

Out of my wrecked marriages
disappointments with friends
the rime time deposits
on heart, imagination

And earth's magnetic pull
downwards to the grave

I want to write poems
as clean and dry
and as impertinent
as this white skull

Found by me
outside the small boneyard
at Mithymna

That perched on a cliffedge
stares
and grins at the sea

ON SEEING THE STATUE OF SAPPHO
ON THE QUAY OF MITYLENE

You look, Sappho,
like one of your own virgins
who has just been told
an off-colour joke
—such a simper

Not at all
as I imagine you
my loving, dark-skinned girl
with yellow hair
and a hand darting
into a man's tunic

No smarter are the citizens
of Mitylene today
than when you showed
yourself in the harbour
to sailors and merchants

Or to the soldier
whose cloak was dyed purple
and was Eros, you said,
on his way down
from heaven

Immortal poetess
you wrote of love
as it no longer is,
of desire without shame

I who have done the same
greet you with the sibylline words
you once sang:
"Dead, I won't be forgotten"
you can have no complaint

But I must go

Aphrodite
has taken care to have
a girl waiting for me
in Mithymna
with soft hands
and softer mouth

She's a sensible girl
and will not mind
if I say the first libation
is to you

Between our raptures
we shall think of you
this night

PROTEST

The church bell clangs
the men and women at once put on
the smiles they've been told
to wear for the occasion
the children get ready to pelt
the great man with flowers
the fat black-bearded priest
walks peaceably beside the mayor

While the Aegean changes colour
they patiently wait

At the agora, however,
the procession will end
and the butcher has hung a solitary
pig's head in his window;
how can the official when he speaks
be kept from seeing
the sly and bloody face
on the black hook

Surely he will have to stare at it
all the time
he's explaining the new constitution:
the great improvements it will bring
to the villagers of Mithymna
called out to cheer him

CREATION

The pregnant cat
rubs her distended belly
against my leg

She moans and stares at me
with simple cat bewilderment
and cannot have enough
of stroking and petting

She arches her back
like a sick voluptuary
to make me extend the caress
I began at her eyes

Saying, and I translate:
"I have earned my moment
and place in Creation;
soon I shall litter life
on this cold dumb ground"

But why suddenly
does she scratch and bite
my stroking hand?

And with so much fury!

SOURWINE SPARKLE

At the exhibition of "Erotica" the faces of the people
who came to stare and conceal their smirks were more
interesting than the explosive genitalia. Pictures and
people seemed to bear an astonishing resemblance to
each other, the men's faces shiny and stretched with
egotism or drooping and wrinkled with failure; the
faces of the women, horsy or vacuously round but
always smug—for this was the female's sanctuary and
achievement—the coldcreamed hollows and creases begging
to be rubbed away by the magical touch of the
extended phallus. In the eyes of both sexes, a terrible
lewdness as if their possessors had just been initiated
into a burdensome secret and were dying for someone
to blurt it out. Yet if that happened how deflated
they would instantly appear. For it is this impure
knowledge, the residue of many unhallowed nights,
which keeps the bags of themselves blown up and
armoured for the day's humiliations. If sex is the wine
of life, as I think it is, in which the ego bathes
and floats and swims in its nectar light and poises
itself joyously between exaltation and extinction,
if it is the unalloyed, self-intoxicating expression of
egotism—the animal flesh with its odours,
secretions and excretions demanding that it be kissed,
caressed, patted and fondled, that is, admired and loved—
what I saw on the faces of the people who crowded up
to the diseased phalli and hairy, black-pit vaginas
was the skin of a wine that had gone sour,
a sourwine sparkle.

HILLS AND HILLS

The hills
remind me
of you

Not because
they curve soft and warm
lovely and firm
under the Greek sun

Or flow
towards the horizon
in slow limpid waves
fading away mysteriously
at the edge of the sea

So that I can only
surmise
their being there
beyond my gaze
and stare into the greyness

But because
a long time ago
you stared at them
as I am staring now

ELEPHANT

Until yesterday I knew nothing about elephants
    except their slowness to mate;
this morning, in a Nepalese village, while I sat out
    the rain in a wayside shrine,
a riderless elephant slowly made his way
    towards one of the ancient trees
lining the street and there began to scrape
    his immense slate-coloured flank
against the rough, knobby bark of a similar greyness
    and toughness; forward and back,
forward and back, as if bent on sawing down the tree
    with one side of his belly;
keeping somehow as much of a clown's sad,
    self-conscious dignity
as humiliating circumstance might allow,
    yet his bull posture
plainly spelling it out: blows, ridicule, men's
                        displeasure
    are wind beneath his ears;
nothing will drive him from this ecstasy rotundity
    and gratuitous weight
make proportionate to his itch, this rapturous blare
    under his vast hide unwrinkling
like a flower.

Look at that wise, old sybarite!
    The creaking tree says it
for him, and the leaves of the tree
    like multiple green tongues:
"A-ah" "A-ah" "A-ah" until the birds
    nesting or resting among them
take it up and translate it into song;
    unhurriedly, methodically
like an old woman washing herself in the morning
    he does the other side of his belly
which now hangs like a big, grey globe of the world;
    then comes the turn

of his nolessitchy behind though his absurd tail
    fouls his sexy stripper's act;
and lastly that of his hind legs, each time making
                                me think
    he has three of them.

He moves his head to let me take in the roguish humour
    in his eyes, the ironic
and quietly exultant smile of someone who has learned
    the necessary art
of converting irritation into pleasure
    and giving a final flick of his tail,
a disdainful yet gentle "that's it" or "that's all
                         for now"
    lumbers off as mysteriously
as he came, leaving me with this poem.

STORM AT YDRA

Blow, blow hard,
Aeolus:
you ask no man's leave

Spit great mouthfuls of water
over the boats
whining like tethered horses,
and crack your long, green fingers,
Neptune, on island walls

Cleanse me, gods,
of the insincerity
learned in cities

Batter the christian lie in my soul;
wash out tolerance and wisdom,
fill my mind with power;
even as you flood
the spaces between the quay's
pavement stones,
pour ecstasy into my breast

Ah, sullen gods,
hurl, heal me with your tempests

ENDS

There is of course
personality

Animals have it too

If you stare
long enough
at a flock of goats
you will notice differences

Or at cows:
one cow's more bovine
than another;
another swings her tail
with nuances of inflection

At sheep, yes, at sheep
and the lambs
Jesus was gentle with

And there is also the mouth
and the large intestine

THE SMELL

Try as hard as he might
to be hero or perfect lover,
the smell of dung
always pursues him

He is dizzy with running;
yet run as fast as he can
past temples and fruit trees
when he stops for breath
the smell is always beside him

On his knees or standing
he prays to the Holy Virgin
to intercede for him.
What's the use?
She too smells: two thousand years
of dysentery

Everything smells of shit.
It surrounds him like a fog
surrounds the lights of the sea-coast;
even the gardens and lanes
are smeared with it,
especially when there are golden sunsets

Nothing defends him
from the monster
burrowing in his nostrils
like a bloated worm

If he buries his head
between the perfumed breasts
of a woman,
he begins to gasp for air
as if he had fallen
into an open latrine

Merciful God
is there no help for this man?
His affliction is greater
than that of lepers
or those shaking wth palsy

Do you hope to pull him
to you
by his nose?
Is the smell your divine hook?

Give it up, Old Man of the Sky.
He has smelled you out too

You, before all others;
you, the first whiff
that came out of his trouser leg
and made his nose
go like a rake over everything

HIS HOLINESS IS RIGHT

I went to the slaughterhouse

It's true

Man
is an animal
                        different
from all the others

FISHERMEN
For Peggy Sylvia

When I wish to make myself perfectly happy
—as happy as when I was an ignorant boy—
I hurry down to the village harbour
to hold in one gaze the sun scarcely above
the horizon, itself a wall of soft flame
and the small brave boats that have been out
all night moving towards the stone pier
stately and slow and magnificent as the ships
of Columbus; O for all their blue solemnity
I think they are bursting to signal us
the great news: "It's been a good haul!"

I have seen fishermen unload their catch;
they are silent with exhaustion, perhaps
with reckoning up their gain. There are still
boxes to fill and broken ice to sprinkle
over the fresh grey skins of the fish
glazing like the eyes of many many-eyed
Arguses crushed and glistening between the crystals;
and the torn nets strung out for mending
when the crates of fish have been nailed shut
—to be freighted to the maritime stomachs
of Athenians waiting for them like ravenous fish.

I like the rhythm and unhurried skill,
the humour and dignity of fishermen.
These are men; they do not have to unravel
Danes and Germans to disinter their dead selves.
Bibliothèques are for the soul-sick, for whoever
have swindled themselves of risk, companions,
the communion of sun and sea. In the monster cities
they are doomed; alas I can summon no pity,
no affection for them: they choose their hell.
Deep and irrational as the sea itself
my joy returns with the fishing boats at dawn.

CLIMBING HILLS

Dictatorship, oppression, fear
what have they to do with me
who sit on a Greek stone by the roadside
staring at the hills ahead and to come,
at the almond and fig trees on both sides
and sometimes straight at the sun
that pins my shadow to the ground
like a burly and invincible wrestler?
Here is peace, the sounds of birds
and insects, sometimes of the wind
but none for too long or too loud;
I am as free as an anarchist
cancelling his self-imposed regulations,
as a nudist when I take down my pants
to ease myself behind a hedge

Here are no doors to knock down,
no persons to placate with smiles
or favours; and I can imagine
all my detractors lying under the blackened
stones of the village cemetery
with all the inscriptions chiselled by me.
It is a good pleasant world, I lack
for nothing. In my mind as I squat
I've wiped out Kosygin and Brehznev
and given the outnumbered Czechs
two hundred divisions with which
to drive the Russian louts back
to the stables they were let loose from,
and before the last grunt I complete
the morning's lofty inspiration
with an amnesty for all the Greeks
in all the prisons Papadopoulos
has made especially large keys for:
he himself has palsy and cannot hold
them, and the secretary to whom
he entrusts them is an underground
spy in the pay of Papandreou
—I mean Andreas, the one with loads

of higher degrees from American
universities and not an ounce
of all-necessary political horse sense

But what's that to me looping my belt
and getting ready to take all those hills
I studied on a map but didn't know
were so numerous or so high?
Still, as long as I can mount them
walking alone with the lantern show
of good and evil only dumb shadows
in my head I don't mind how many they are.
Hills are so sane, so honourable
with the sunlight straddling them,
and won't suddenly rear up to throw you
into a ditch; hills don't set traps
either, are not treacherous and will not
accept bribes to tell lies;
I've never known one of them ever
try to deceive me or to menace my welfare:
a neighbour threatened to kill my child

So I like hills, especially with gravelled
roads running through them; and I can say
for roads what I just said about hills;
they seem made for each other,
like some old couples one meets up with
before one's too old himself and lucky:
particularly this morning with a soft
breeze at my back and the sun holding
in reserve his full strength until I reach
the village at the top of the last hill.
After that I'll sit with a bottle of retsina
and think of Kosygin and Brehznev again
and of Papadopoulos whom I left way back
several turns and hedges ago
and of a world as tranquil and lovely
as the hours when together with the sun
I mounted these radiant hills.

NEPALESE WOMAN AND CHILD

Poets have easy tears
for what they imagine
is your predicament:
tears but no solutions

And Switzerland exports
like wristwatches and cheese
nice-smelling, intelligent women
to teach you their unhappiness

Demagogues with cold eyes
advance on your crumbling doorstep
to amplify your sigh
into a peal of thunder

Time doubtless has griefs stored up
for you dazed and gross as the earth
and your tiny son that hangs
like a black pendant under your chin

Smoke your hookah forever
and give suck to your baby
O perfect symbol
of stupor and fertility

HOLOCAUST

Each morning he finds at the sink myriads of tiny
brown insects—a mass of virile pencil dots—
merging and diverging. Where did they come from?
He stares at the unanswering marble top and
surrounding tiled walls. By contrast with the
restless insects they seem more inert, more than ever
mere philistine matter. Momentarily he warms up
to the skirmishing armies massed on the rim of the
sink, the abyss. His daily ontological lesson.
Nothingness hell-bent for nowhere. Godlike he
observes for a few moments this ridiculous parody
on human existence, sponge in hand. No angel parts
the ceiling to shout, "Hold!" And with one rough
sweep he wipes away this living smear of fig-jam
(including one or two artists and philosophers
who have separated themselves from the frothing
brown mass) and restores to the marble top its
cold ironical surface.

ISRAELIS

It is themselves they trust and no one else;
Their fighter planes that screech across the sky,
Real, visible as the glorious sun;
Riflesmoke, gunshine, and rumble of tanks.

Man is a fanged wolf, without compassion
Or ruth: Assyrians, Medes, Greeks, Romans,
And devout pagans in Spain and Russia
—Allah's children, most merciful of all.

Where is the Almighty if murder thrives?
He's dead as mutton and they buried him
Decades ago, covered him with their own
Limp bodies in Belsen and Babi Yar.

Let the strong compose hymns and canticles,
Live with the Lord's radiance in their hard skulls
Or make known his great benevolences;
Stare at the heavens and feel glorified

Or humbled and awestruck buckle their knees:
They are done with him now and forever.
Without a whimper from him they returned,
A sign like an open hand in the sky.

The pillar of fire: Their flesh made it;
It burned briefly and died—you all know where.
Now in their own blood they temper the steel,
God being dead and their enemies not.

AFTER AUSCHWITZ

My son,
don't be a waffling poet;
let each word you write
be direct and honest
like the crack of a gun

Believe an aging poet
of the twentieth century:
neither the Old Testament
nor the New
or the sayings of the Koran
or the Three Baskets of Wisdom
or of the Dhammapada
will ever modify or restrain
the beastliness of men

Lampshades
were made from the skins
of a people
preaching the gospel of love;
the ovens of Auschwitz and Belsen
are open testimony
to their folly

Despite memorial plaques
of horror and contrition
repentance, my son,
is short-lived;
an automatic rifle, however,
endures
a lifetime

THE FINAL PEACE

I lift up my arms
to pluck tranquillity
from the hills and trees

I scoop it out of the sea,
letting the silver-white coins
fall back into the sea

I want nothing in my hand
but water and sunlight
—a fist cannot hold them

Why should I contend with anyone?
Surely Death is his enemy
as he is mine

SILENT JOY

Remembering
St. James street, Sunday mornings
—a vast empty cathedral,
my footsteps echoing in the silent vaults

rooms on quiet afternoons, alone
or with one I loved deeply

shadows, cool and long, in hot lanes

insect-humming cemeteries
and light dripping from vines
in globules of rose, of pale-green

I am so utterly filled
with joyful peace and wonder,
my heart stops beating

Friends, I stare at everything
with wide, with sightless eyes
like one who has just died

LEAVETAKING

Good-bye
fields, waves, hills, trees
and fairweather birds whose blasts
woke me each morning at dawn

So that I might see
the early sun

Good-bye, Sun

I am growing older
I must instruct myself to love you all
with moderation

May you be as kind
to the next poet
who comes this way
as you have been to me

When you see him,
give him my felicitations
and love

POSTSCRIPT TO EMPIRE

Behind Connaught Place
shops, buildings, houses
look like platoons of exhausted soldiers
after a forced march in the sun

And at the intersection
of Parliament and Viceroy or Parliament and Curzon
Hindus, seeing me, speak only English
—just like the Fr. Canadians back home

And the manager of the hotel where I stay
wishes to know when Memsahib is coming,
and certainly the editor of Times of India
is a re-incarnation of Steele or Macaulay

And a sign at the famous Aryan temple
sternly prohibits the passing of urine
on the premises; also Christians
and Moslems on all the holy days

And each night dark-skinned young men
detach themselves from the shadows
to whisper old perversities in my ear:
their voices are soft as the tread of pumas

And the nights, black as India ink,
are filled with the cries of vanquished conquerors,
of gods and beasts and men become like beasts;
I listen and do not know what to think

For in the intense white light of day
the bicycles that lie neatly sprawled in dusty lots
have the air of bicycles that are waiting
for the *Wille Zur Macht* to mount them and ride away

BUGS

Whenever
I see bugs manoeuvring
on the kitchen floor
with bits of food or paper
sticking to their bodies

I have a resistless desire
to crush them
under my foot

Only if they have bright colours
will I spare them

IF EUCLID WERE YOUR ANALYST

Man
is the only animal
that finds pain sweet:
of other preferably;
his own,
if he's a modern masochist

He is also
the only animal
that extols and creates
beauty—consciously
Ergo: art
is the enjoyment
of cruelty
without the infliction
of pain. Q.E.D.

POMEGRANATES

Thank you, John and Julie
for the pomegranates

That was nice of you

In the heat
one of them split
right down the centre;
the other didn't

They reminded me
of two sisters
I once knew

CHANGELING

In my arms
you become again
a Russian

Germany
your neat one-and-a-half room apt.
in West Berlin
your work for the newspapers
drop in quiet folds around the bed

Your pubis
is a warm granary
in the white bareness of your body

I watch the gradual return
of your homeland
in the midnight blooming of your breasts,
in the transformation
of your mouth and chin: the primness
all gone

Your laugh
is a sunlit Ukrainian wheatfield;
your kisses are music
coming unexpectedly from behind
closed windows

More than half your life
lies in ruin

As summoning the lust
of a young Tolstoy
and sentences
from our favourite Russian
authors
I drive into you again and again

from *Nail Polish*

RECIPE FOR A LONG AND HAPPY LIFE

Give all your nights
to the study of Talmud

By day practise
shooting from the hip

THE HAUNTING

Why without cease do I think of a bold youth
    national origin unimportant or racial Peruvian
Russian Irish Javanese he has fine clear eyes
honest smiling mouth a pat for a child's head
talks to old women and helps them cross the street
    is friendly with mainliners anarchs and nuns
Cote St. Luc housewives their ruined husbands and brats
optometrists sign painters lumpenproletarians dumping
their humps into coffee cups plotting revenge
and clerics who've made out of Christ a bearded faggot

From the rotating movement of a girl's beautiful
    buttocks he draws energy as from the sun
(O lovely revolving suns on St. Catherine street)
and from breasts and perfumed shoulders and hair
Picadilly Wilhelmstrasse Fifth Avenue Rue St. Germain
    the suns go rolling on luminous hoops pinwheels
handsprings and somersaults of desirable flesh
the bold youth with wide-apart happy eyes
stepping lightly over blossoming asphalt graves is running
after them touching a child's head smiling to old women

Why don't I ever meet him face to face?
    sometimes I've seen him stepping off a bus
but when I've caught up with him he's changed
into a bourgeois giving the two-fingered peace sign
or a poet shouting love as if it were a bomb
    on damp days into an office clerk smelling of papers
is he somebody's doppelganger? an emanation or
shadow I see taking shape near a plateglass window?
who is he? he haunts me like an embodied absence
and as if I had lived all my life in arrears

FOR ANNA

You wanted the perfect setting
for your old world beauty, postwar Hungarian:
a downtown Toronto bar sleazy
with young whores pimps smalltime racketeers

remembering boyhood Xmases in Elmira
plus one poet pissed to the gills
by turns raving or roaring like an acidhead
then suddenly silent like the inside of a glass

I'm sure you placed him there as camera
as incorruptible juror or witness
but who can give report of a miracle?
having seen it what struck dumb can he tell?

and to whom? they who pressed around you
were converted and left off dreaming of murder
or rape in public parks/some cried for happiness . . .
they outside or riding the subways will never believe

Now I know everything which happened
that night was your creation/you invented
it all by cupping your elegant proper hands
then letting the night escape like a black moth

that shattered the fantastic radiance of your head
into a thousand glints and scintillations
transfiguring bottles whisky glasses even the leers
on aroused Canadian clerks fingering their wallets

and making me run after you to discover
whether you are a woman with blood and orifices
one may after all love and if the answer is yes
whether you will warm my aging limbs as a lover

THE GARDENER

he lives life without fuss
or explanations
                cutting grass, trimming
trees and hedges
                an octogenarian's soundness
in all his motions

half-French, half-English
of the two solitudes
he's made one large tranquillity
of acceptance
                and has never listened
for the bitter songs
wounded self-love hums
                in the ear
of impotence and defeat

wanting no man's pity or compassion
least of all
            of poets pandering
to their own weakness
                only
the remaining strength
in his seven good fingers
            disease
hasn't twisted
            into black unfeeling claws
and the bite of a solitary tooth
standing firm
            in his jaw
like a weatherbeaten nail
for his smile to hang on

DIONYSOS IN HAMPSTEAD

Springtime's greensickness squirrels
and insects roiled soiled coiled
in cycles of propagation and death
tender blossoms of apple rough winds staple
to the heavy false odours of lilac
and dung my neighbour's disciplined lawns

I shout hooray for everything that dances
wild songs fucking birds and beasts wild words
an Australasian waving her gay pirate's flag
of pubic hair her snakelike arms writhing
over breasts and crotch O Florentine whores
with gestures of great lewdness and beauty

The wise and the just are too solemn
under their long shadows they do not dance
at the weddings I hear in the grass
at the mock funerals I hear in the leaves of trees
and hedges sunlight trims with golden razors
they do not leapfrog in ancient cemeteries

Who am I to explain sovereignty and flowers
who forever am thinking of silent unseen cracks
music makes till all walls fall in slowly
dissolving dreams of the migrations of birds
and terrorists the bad poets of this century
laying their heads like bombs between a woman's thighs

On a rock surrounded by alligators and goats
I sit shedding invisible blossoms like dreams
over quiet archipelagos and Africas
more content than an old astrologer
who belches from a surfeit of stars and charts
till heaven's sceneshifter arrives and
covers the earth with a bloodstained shroud

I CAN SLEEP BESIDE MY LADY

Wolves mutilated my lady
her glory dripped from their tongues
and flamed upon the snow
O they rolled her naked body
where the ditch received her limbs
like a swollen powdered crease

But green and velvet was the night
and all her lovers
were marooned in the movies
while the lovers of her lovers
gossiped about sparrows
in the Northeastern Lunch

I who might have saved her
watched instead
her bright blood spill on snow
I who might have saved her
was hungry for the whisper
of her matted hair

And all the houses kneel
like bloated nuns in prayer
around my love they kneel
remote as David's ships
or sway like weak and fasting saints
as she lies bleeding there
from her damaged fingerprints

O rabbis and angels
and lovers marooned
forever in lost movies
when wind and wolves have had their fill
I shall unstitch the clawmarks
from my lady's lovely flesh
I shall sleep all night
beside her bruised and glistening body
on a lonely hill

AS SEEN THROUGH A GLASS DARKLY

Armoured
archaic
and looking
like a man-of-war
in a naval museum
—an old furious dreadnought
manoeuvring into line
in, say, a famous forgotten film
about imperial England

One crimson, cruising
lobster
on the aquarium floor
finally settles stiffly
alongside another

Each moves with slow deliberate
courtesy
keeping temper and pride
under admirable control,
like a retired major-general
I imagine escorting
his youngest daughter
to the theatre box

Nevertheless
for all their upperclass formality
lobsters
in a restaurant aquarium
remind me vividly
of communist and socialist friends

Could it be it's their colour
—a half-boiled red?

No: rather
it's the appearance lobsters
in their safe cubicles give
of a rectitude overstressed
because unnatural,
of party earnestness and conviction,
of seeming—that's it!—too self-conscious
exponents
of Kant's categorical imperative

While whatever-one-calls-them,
their feeding filaments,
make small currents of water
and insignificant
bubbles
that break
on coming to the top
without the expected pop

PLEA FOR MY LADY

You won't let me kiss you?
Me?

Lady, you must be joking!
Lady, you must be mad!

Who put the agony in my lips
as though they had sucked
for a thousand years
on a prickly pear?

Who taught them
to want yours
with such a fever?
On crowded thoroughfares
of the city
I feel my mouth pulled
towards wherever you are.
Mariners need a compass.
You are my lodestar.

Of what use are my hands
if you won't let them caress you?
My arms, if they can't embrace you?
O my whole frame's
become a piece of useless junk.

The season that lovers
and worms wait for
is here
but your disdain
has sewn up all my senses
with invisible threads.

I'm blind to green buds
dead to lilac smells
deaf to all birdsongs.

I can't, O lady, even hear
my own cries
wilder than those Abelard
shrieked
that wild night
they plucked out his stones.

Lady, let me have your lips
Lady, let my hands caress you
Lady, let me embrace you
O lady, lady, lady, lady

END OF THE WHITE MOUSE

I do not know what Chinese dragons eat
but *vipera russellii* in cages must be fed

On the soft mat of vipershit, godlike,
without compassion or malice
the famed nutritionist
released the white mouse
—cotton fluff with bright pink eyes—
and for a second only
the poor albino
turned to us his bewildered pink eyes
then shifted and ran around the cage
—the dancing, prancing little show-off;
ran with the heady stuff of life
in his ridiculous tiny wishbone legs,
at times raising himself against the glass cage,
standing there, white, like a splayed bat,
then fluttering off into the flecked shadows,
a piece of cambric in a sudden lift of air

Stung,
the white mouse reared up,
swayed and wobbled like a diapered infant
—the death quiver in his small buttocks—
then fell like a furred stone,
the four legs stiffening with eternity

The unhinged viper
swallowed him head first
and the last I saw of the mouse
was a poignant good-bye flick of his tail,
the soothing peristalsis
ending only when he rested
in the middle of the viper's length:
a pleasant, elastic, cosy bubble
lulling as the Madonna's lap after the Annunciation

And I broke into laughter
for this absurdity
and for the mouse's juices soon to begin
running the length and roundness of the viper,
for the flesh and fragile bones commencing
their inevitable transformative cellular dance

I laughed
as might any well-disciplined Zarathustrian
in this godless epoch
but that evening after I'd sown grass seed
in the round bald spot of my lawn
neatly circular as Caesar's empty pate,
restored the earth and watered it carefully,
suddenly when I was resting on the doorstep
I felt a tremor in my head and frame
as if a whole world had moved inside me

SHAKESPEARE

My young son asks me:
"who's the greatest poet?"
Without any fuss I say, Shakespeare.
"Is he greater than you?"
I ho-ho around that one
and finally give a hard "yes."
"Will you ever be greater
than . . . a splatter of lisped S's
and P's . . . ?"
I look up at my son
from the page I'm writing on:
he too wants his answer
about the greatness of Shakespeare
though only six and carefree;
and I see with an amused hurt
how my son has begun to take on
one of those damned eternal fixtures
of the human imagination
like "God" or "Death" or "the start
of the world"; along with these
it'll be with him the rest
of his life like the birthmark
on his right buttock; so as though
I were explaining God or Death
I say firmly without a trace
of ho-ho in my voice: No, I'll never
be greater than William Shakespeare,
the world's greatest poetic genius
that ever will be or ever wuz
hoping my fair-minded admission
won't immediately blot out
the my-father-can-lick-anyone image
in his happy ignorant mind
and take the shine away
that's presently all around my head.
That unclimbable mountain, I rage;
that forever unapproachable star
pulsing its eternal beams from a far

stillness onto our narrow screens
set up as Palomar libraries and schools
to catch the faintest throb of light.
Damn that unscalable pinnacle
of excellence mocking our inevitable
inferiority and failure
like an obscene finger; a loud curse
on the jeering "beep . . . beeps"
that come from dark silence
and outer galactic space to unscramble
into the resonant signature of
"Full many a glorious morning" or
"The quality of mercy is not strained"
or "Out, out, brief candle . . ."
NO poet for all time, NO poet
till this planet crack into black night
and racking whirlwinds EVER
to be as great as William Shakespeare?
My God, what a calamitous burden
far worse than any horla or incubus:
a tyrant forever beyond the relief
of bullet or pointed steel . . .
What a terrible lion in one's path!
What a monumental stone
in the constrictive runnel of anyone
with an itch to write great poems
—and poets so cursed beyond all
by vanity, so loused up in each inch
of their angry, comfortless skin
with the intolerable twitch of envy!
Well, there's nothing to be done
about that bastard's unsurpassable
greatness; one accepts it like cancer
or old age, as something that one
must live with, hoping it will prod us on
to alertest dodges of invention
and circumvention, like the brave spider
who weaves his frail home in the teeth
of the lousiest storm and catches
the morning sun's approving smile;

Anyhow there's one saving grace:
that forever smiling damned bastard,
villain, what-have-you, is dead
and no latest success of his
can embitter our days with envy,
paralyze us into temporary impotency,
despair rotting our guts and liver;
yes, though the greatest that ever wuz
or ever will be he's dead, dead,
and all the numerous flattering busts
keep him safely nailed down
among the worms he so often went raving
on about when his great heart burst
and all the griefs of the world
came flooding out. His ghost may wander
like Caesar's into my tent
by this rented lake, and I'll entertain
him; but he must also stand outside
begging for entry when I keep his volume
shut, and then he's out in the cold
like his own poor Lear. And—well—
there's my six-year-old son
who says of the clothes flapping
on the clothesline: "Look, they're
scratching themselves," or compares
his mother's nipples to drain-plugs
he says he wishes to pull out, or
tells me the rain is air crying
—and he only four at the time;
and though I swear I never told him
of Prospero and his great magic
asked me the other day: "Is the world real?"
So who really can tell, maybe one day
one of my clan will make it
and there'll be another cock-of-the-walk,
another king-of-the-castle; anyway
we've got our bid in, Old Bard.

CEMETERIES

Cemeteries
        are thrown away
on North Americans
they behave
        as if they are going
to live forever
          ignoring
in their walks and car-drives
these discreet dumps
with their sad embarrassed slabs
that advertise
        human refuse

Yet death's certain ignominy's
the one sure pull of sanity
and eternity
        in their lives
a tranquil interlude
          in the senseless ceaseless
biological froth
  where finally and mercifully
there are no answers
          and no lies
no absurd rebellion
but—shattering paradox—dignity
and, as bonus, rest

ARAN ISLANDS

Dun Aengus

High walls . . . of stones;
man-humbling cliff and shattering sea;
ramparts:
trenches of stone, fierce four of them
and in-between
prehistory's barbed wire, *cheveux de frise*
. . . of stones.

Enclosing a mist.

Gone are the defenders;
gone, they who attacked.

Nothing here:
only mist
and blue-grey stones.

Cliffs of Moher

At last, as in a dream,
I've come to the cliffs
from where God hurls down
his enemies, every one.

Rat-faced cunning mercers
with a rat's delight;
all, all who are dead of soul,
male and female.

See, their polls open like flowers
on the black rocks below;
their brains dance with the foam
on a green wave's tow.

Kilmurvey

Low are the hills, a mere rise
in the ground, grey with stones and green;
Stand anywhere and you can trace
outlines with your new-found eyes
of stone fences delicate as lace:
Stand anywhere and you can be seen.

OSIP MANDELSHTAM (1891-1940)

I once did an hour-long TV show reading
from your *Stamen* and *Tristia*: out there
were my compatriots who had never before
heard of your name and pain, your nightmare fate;
of course the impressario spoke impressively
about your stay in Paris where you mastered
the French symbolists, your skill as translator
(what pre-Belsen Jew hadn't promiscuously
shacked up with five or six gentile cultures)
the Hellenic feeling in your prose and poems
—to be brief, he filled in the familiar picture
of enlightened Jew ass bared to the winds

But when that self-taught master symbolist
il miglior fabbro put you on his list of touchables
that was the end; you perished in the land waste
of Siberia, precisely where no one knows and few care
for in that stinking imperium whose literature
you adorned like a surrealist Star of David
you're still an unclaimed name, a Jewish ghost
who wanders occasionally into enclaves
of forlorn intellectuals listening
for the ironic scrape of your voice
in the subversive hum of underground presses

I know my fellow-Canadians, Osip;
they forgot your name and fate as swiftly
as they learned them, switching off
the contorted image of pain with their sets,
choosing a glass darkness to one which starting
in the mind covers the earth in permanent eclipse;
so they chew branflakes and crabmeat gossip make love
take out insurance against fires and death
while our poetesses explore their depressions
in delicate complaints regular as menstruation
or eviscerate a dead god for metaphors;
the men-poets displaying codpieces of wampum,
the safer legends of prairie Indian and Eskimo

Under a sour and birdless heaven
TV crosses stretch across a flat Calvary
and plaza storewindows give me
the blank expressionless stare of imbeciles:
this is Toronto, not St. Petersburg on the Neva;
though seas death and silent decades separate us
we yet speak to each other, brother to brother;
your forgotten martyrdom has taught me scorn
for hassidic world-savers without guns and tanks:
they are mankind's gold and ivory toilet bowls
where brute or dictator relieves himself
when reading their grave messages to posterity
—let us be the rapturous eye of the hurricane
flashing the Jew's will, his mocking contempt for slaves

OHMS

ohms
is such a beautiful word

soft as marshmallow in the mouth
as a lover's sigh

hearing it for the first time
in Physics 6
I was electrified

it was like my first kiss
my first piece of ass
but cleaner purer

since then I've loved ohms
passionately
especially ohms of resistance

if you try to say the word
in anger
or vindictively
you can't ohms is pure poetry

bellow it
it comes out a muted cry of pain:
the sound the universe makes

yet poets have written
about owls yes about owls many times

nightingales snakes daffodils bridges
graveyards
but not about ohms

therefore I've written this poem
and now wish to add only this:

ohms is immortal
chaste and lovely as a rainbow
it will delight our seed
on Venus Jupiter Mars

when the great Florentine
even he
is gibberish to their ears

FOR NATALYA CORREIA

You possess the sturdy elegance of a cannon
and move always with the authority
of someone about to capture a city

Are indisputably beyond the vanity
of attention and compliments
like famous statues fixed in permanent triumph

Who in aloof approving silence
or unending melancholy disdain
regard their admirers at the crowded base

If you dispense anger or annoyance
it is as if doing so you establish
the existence of those who provoked them

And entertain each day those certainties
acclamation and gratified desire foster
in a voluptuous and talented woman

I admire wholeheartedly the egotism
with which you half stretch out on your couch
like a glistening female sealion

And pour without my permission
wine from my wineglass into your own
fanning with delighted self-absorption

The smoke curling about your impressive head
or jab into space your ebony cigaret holder
as if to poke emeralds from their hiding place

ETERNAL RECURRENCE

Even that leaf as it falls
Will one day fall again
Be sad, be gaily crimson
And flutter while a bird calls

And the bough on which he sits
Lengthen into the dark
While my staring eyes mark
How between the trees your shadow flits

And in my mind image of your face
Vain and angry as you said
Your words and turned away your head:
They will come again, the pain and grace

A million years hence; and from that bough
The same bird calling,
The same crimson leaf falling
And I writing and weeping—then as now

KILMURVEY STRAND

An old man walks barefoot
in the water his trousers
rolled up to his knees
and his hair is white
as the foam is white He
bends his shape to hear
the seagulls crying overhead
and scatter the fragments
of cloud floating in the stilled
pools he wades into between
the rocks
        In the vortex
of his happiness he revolves
like an uprooted plant in
a small remote whirlpool lend-
ing a small dignity to its suck
All his years are pebbles under
his feet Sands on the fine hairs
of his blueveined calves

The waves pick up
sand and brown mice
sometimes huge black rats They
do it over and over
one more time till doomsday
with the same patient roar
of admonition but the mice
and black rats keep dissolving

One white cloud then another
each nudging the other
over humps lustreless aeons
of hills have reared

I kneel on the strand
and notice things unhelpful
for myself at fifty-seven
still capable of hope
and anger no thought of mine
pushed from behind but appear-
ing as if from nowhere like
a bird solitary and sudden
in a sky one
had not noticed before

LAKE SELBY

Definitely it's not polluted
since no germ would wish
to be found dead in it,
and also it's absolutely
safe for you and the kids
for however far you walk
into its lukewarm wetness
wavelets sedulously suck-suck
at your hips and navel: believe me
it's hardly worth trying
to drown in it; you'd only
be found sitting on your bottom
and the lake's, rope around
your neck or ankle,
stone heavy in your lap

My son who is six flatly
refuses to swim in it
though wind and water
drive him crazy with joy,
especially water;
he calls the stuff squishing
through his toes "sea food"
and wants none of its sliminess;
as he describes it
it's so many vile fingers
clutching clammily at his heels
he has to kick at furiously
before they will release him
sputtering with rage
and spitting out mouthfuls
of tepid lakewater and weeds

Yet the townsmen summering it
in stolid painted cottages
that each year tighten
around the lake like a noose
plunge into the shallow water
with cries of delight and gusto
ha-ha-ing to one another
and trying a hundred-and-one tricks
to amuse the less venturesome on shore;
for hours and hours I watch them
pretend they're bouncing porpoises
leviathans and comical octopi
or cruel-mouthed sharks
to make their beached wives and progeny
wave admiringly and praise;
afterwards, scrubbed clean of grime
and slime, smoking their pipes
they will sit and stare at the lake
which moon and silence have changed
into a silvered apparition
or some lost and perfect island
rising slowly to enchant them
between the dark elms and pines

ENTRY

He was a Jew with a faked identity
card;
the ghetto was in flames, its puny defenders
scattered, dead

As he crossed the emptied square of the now
silent city
and looking up saw the great
black cathedral of Warsaw
the immovable stars overhead
he was caught suddenly
in the murderous crossfire of nazi and partisan guns

He hugged the bloodstained rubbish and stones
and laughed into the dark at how
an impersonal death by a willed or stray bullet
made one at last a human among humans

ABSENCE

Love,
I make a silence
out of your name
and dip
my hands into it

LAURA CUNNEYFLOW

returning from her summer travels
—an event annual
as ploughing & seeding—
Laura at once tells me
of the men who tried to lay her,
of their near-triumphs and failures
—and of their triumphs!
I listen to her
entranced
since life-loving
middle-aged chicks
wall-to-walling
in plush vacation hotels
on the beaches
of Nice and Havana
have much to teach
a melancholy poet

chemically pure redhead bubble
in the ceaseless senseless
biological froth
Laura Cunneyflow rich
and riggish
mistfully remembering
the vast innocence
of her lovers
in four continents,
their endearing romanticism,
is a portent
on whose entrails
the future has already
begun to move

from *Lovers and Lesser Men*

TIDE

Lovers
and lesser men
have gone on and on
endlessly and persuasively

About the anguished
half-choked
sputtering cry
the circumscribed tide
makes—its hiss
and last sigh—
before it collapses
on the white sand
and dies

I note only
what happens
to the bright refractions
of light

When the dashed water
lies momentarily low
slow-moving and still
on its dull supporting porous table

FORTUNA ET CUPIDAS

Appetite and chance, luck and desire·
together make a man's fate
not the foolish lines on his palm nor the conjugation
of stars in space rule his lot
but these intangible bars infrangibly up and down
on which if he pleases he can graph his days
until he falls from their arching bough
like a ripe fruit to rot or burn

But a man's ball spins merrily merrily
in the roulette wheel of sexuality
at last comes to rest in a gay groove
red black black red fifteen or fifty-one
to the bored indifferent croupier it is all one
scramble your gamble, ramble and gambol
the appointed groove hole slot is always there
waiting for the balls to come tumbling in

Only a few have the guts to shoot themselves
outside where the despair of the casinos
is a sighing fragrance among the leaves and flowers
when the luck has been consistently bad
and all is lost, even that lovely fire
that flamed and flared in thighs and testicles
but at home the defeated roam from room to room
or run from corridors that come running after them

Or hunt for weapons that will let them stay,
the sharp remorse-killing knife and loaded gun
to finger lovingly and to put away;
of one dubious luck the poet alone is lord
good or bad let the gods who flay him say:
to find a memorable name for his anguish
a fat phrase for his woe or a rhyme for the crime
when fortune reloads her glass and carefully takes aim

My youth will not come again
let my gaze be that of the sun, a bold eye
in a bright blue sky, a Greek sky and high
high over the riotous men and women who dance
to the clanging tunes of appetite and chance;
other gods for other men, idols or frauds; mine
be only these to the end of my stubborn days
mine be the brave grateful heart to give them praise

FAREWELL

She's gone. The one I swore up and down
to give a Greek villa and six children
if she married me, a trip around the world
to the moon, Mars, Venus
anywhere so that I could be with her
so great was the fire in my head,
in the sleeved arms that ached to hold her.

She's gone. The one that made me turn
restlessly from side to side each
sleepless night, thinking of her cool naked limbs
curled up on the lovestained sheets,
her red lips and long black lashes,
her smiles, her pouts, her sexy gestures,
the perfection of her small feet.

She's gone, whose laughter made me forget
the decorum of grey hairs,
children, friends, literary foes
the importance of being Trudeau, Pompidou, Spiro Agnew
or even the illustrious dust of Uncle Ho.
Let the whole world be damned, I said
and let the dead marry off the dead.

She's gone in whose arms I rose
resurrected after the third lay;
peace and wild joy and laughter were mine
for awhile but she's gone, gone in a bus
that with a snort has taken her far away
while the grey dust that settles over me
swirls and twirls like the ghost of an empty day.

RUPERT BROOKE
1887-1915

Great lover, your sweetness is lost forever
thought and discourse being, alas, much rougher
than when you were alive and wrote: but I've seen
your tomb and naked un-English statue, your ass
your bronze ass turned to the sea—I wonder why

I would have had you facing it, staring down
its famous inquietude as a poet should
though listening always to its many voices
nor would I have stuck that ridiculous scroll
in your hand. Rupert, I think the sculptor

Greek no doubt modelled you on the 'Discus Thrower'
or 'Apollo Belevedere', put in inspired splashes
of both and made your exquisite Saxon head
too small for the classical legs and torso.
The thing's a mess and that's the brazen truth.

Yet though the sun was hot and high over
Skyros I mounted the hill wanting to see
your tomb and statue for a schoolboy once
in Baron Byng I memorized your sonnet which begins
'If I should die think only this of me. . . .'

And this morning in the Hotel Xenia I recited
all of it to my girl over a *portokalada*.
So you're not quite dead though your great fame
will not come back again. No matter poet and lover
of inns and chinaware, of quiet country lanes

Though the brute world in the shape of this gravel truck
has thrust itself under your moulded genital,
quit of phony accent, the mannered phrase, your hang-up
with language and beauty comes through—the poet's
timeless eponym none can fake or erase.

Skyros, Greece
June 14, 1972

STELLA

All afternoon she sits in the doorway, a tourist attraction
    to be stared at by Greeks or the foreigners
Who know her story. Old and ill and her feet swollen
    to rhinoceros size
Once, long ago, she was a wild creature so fair and disdainful
    she made the sober merchants dream at their tills
And fishermen haul in lascivious sea-nymphs all night long.
Their wives, even the comeliest of virgins, cursed her beauty
    praying their merciful God
To strike her with plague or leprosy. One day He lifted a petitioner's
    taper from its tiny brass socket
And turned it into a man handsome and clever with words, poet
    and talked-about novelist from another island.
She saw him and fell, his curious fire loosening her limbs;
In the crumbling Genoese castle, surrounded by ears, they made love.
The furious villagers rejoiced. At last the contemptuous beauty
    had been roiled in the mire
Her scented petticoats pulled over her head, her besmutted buttocks
    for all to see.
O the fetid dreams of men! How they besmeared the white breasts
    that had made them groan in their sleep
How they reviled what for so long they had longed for in vain
While the women and girls so lit up the church with grateful candles
    you'd think for weeks God's face was shining there.
He lifted yet another taper and blew out its flame: the teller of tales
    made off for Athens to compose
A moving novel about their tragic love and never saw her again
But overnight she became the ruined unhappy heroine of a thousand
    lustful dreams
Such that aesthetes and bored rich women dream and wandered from
    place to place to return at last comfortless and impenitent
To her village and the filthy leers of men, the compassionate jeers
    of wives and virgins
To live solitary and infamous in the house where you see her now.

All that was long ago. Day by remorseless day her famed and troubling
      beauty crumbled into commemorative moles,
      wrinkles and yellowing parchment skin
And the heartbreak of an old woman's toothless grin.
Now there isn't a villager, old or young, who doesn't run up to embrace
      this hairy misshapen crone
      with the wild gone look in her eyes
And the sour excremental smell that fills up her doorway.
Not one who does not feel glad and right having someone whom daily
      he can forgive and pity
Or whose heart is not made proud to fix her hoary and humbled at the end
      of his benevolent stare;
Especially since the government itself is rumoured to allow her
      a small stipend to sit in the doorway
      to be gawked at, an Aeschylean lesson for all Greeks,
Her fabled loveliness caught forever in a work of imperishing art
      while her dying decrepit self,
A tourist attraction in the village, puts still more drachmas
      in the merchants' tills.

Molibos, Greece
July 21, 1972

I THINK OF OVID

I think of Ovid and the merry twinkle
in his eyes as he fingerfucks the dressed-to-kill
matron sitting beside him while her husband
facing them on the opposite side of the table
feelingly descants on Plato's ION
—he's no fool that man, knows a thing or two
about the arts, is even flattered by the famous poet's
attentions to his wife—and the other guests,
a noted critic of plays among them, a Proconsul
just returned from Alexandria and a clutch
of minor poets cutting their envious teeth
on Virgil's shanks but plainly intending Ovid's,
bare their teeth in vinous approbation. The husband
is very obviously pleased with himself
and the unexpected impression he's made on everyone.
His wife is beautiful, the much-sought-after Ovid
is sitting at her side, filling her glass
and paying her compliments that are making
her squirm and giggle with laughter.
It's a scene that would move anyone
always tuned-in like himself to what's significant
and meaningful in this wretched world
and always eager to seize whatever enjoyments
it keeps locked up in its hidden storeroom.
His educated mind calls the live composition
in front of him *Beauty and Fame* but swiftly
changes it round out of deference to Ovid's
greatness. He's touched to discover so much
sensibility in himself, such a quick and lively mind
—true, his host has not been stingy
with his best Falernian and the guests
have been attentive, even flattering
to the provincial pair though his good-looking wife
would win the heart of Caesar himself,
the old curmudgeon—and so he lets himself go,
pulls out all the stops and speaks with unwonted
persuasive eloquence and warmth, with real passion
about *poesis*, glancing at the renowned poet
from time to time to see how he's making out,

whether his words have been winged with divine fire.
Meanwhile Ovid all evening has been keeping up
a steady pressure on the proud matron's clit,
stroking it gently, using only one finger
—the experienced lecher—till he feels a gush
of cuntjuice, warm and viscous, suffuse
his finger and run down his wearied hand.
Only now does he smile to the moist-eyed husband
whom emotion has finally choked up. He smiles
approvingly, genially; he smiles from a full heart,
knowing that in an uncertain world
where death and a woman's scheming hypocrisy
are the only things a sensible man will bank on,
and men are black-hearted and joyless,
the cold lusts of money and position solely
exciting them, the gods approve an innocent
fingerfuck giving pleasure to himself and the lady
and making her come—decorously as the occasion
required; and that this or the real thing itself
(screw the fine things promised by dictator or sage)
is a mortal good within our mortal means
before we join the joyless shades of Hell.

AN AUBADE

It is early morning.
The cocks have stopped crowing.
The villagers are waking from dreams
of religious exaltation and buggery.
In their heads while shaving
or stirring their coffee
they carefully lock up their schemes
for profit and cuckoldry.
At the approach of this band of light
men arise to cheat or murder.
O wondrous Light! O wondrous Sun!
It has brought back their colours
to cowsheds and gardenias
to chickens and village dogs
who begin to squawk and bark
at their strange appearance.
From faraway mournful fields
the asses are braying,
"We want wimmin. We want wimmin."
On the road the pellets of goatshit
look like stunted olives.
In other lands it is dark, dark.
North Ireland, Vietnam.
There light explodes like a bomb
or comes upon the night
like an assassin.
I sit on my bed and light a cigarette.
My girl is still sleeping.
When she awakes how will I
who read Husserl and Camus
tell her of my simple need of her
and that she must never leave me?

POETRY AND TRUTH

Poets err or they lie.
Poems do not give us truth but
Reveal like lightning the
Forked road that leads us to it.

THAT IS THE QUESTION

In Skyros
under a fine unclouded sky
in the company
of cheerful relaxed people
who do not own a pot to piss in
I am certain
Toronto does not exist,
being less real than vanished Troy or Delphi

Returned home
to grey streets and greyer people
who lock their hearts
for safe-keeping in vaults and boxes
and regard me
with cold suspecting eyes
I am persuaded Toronto exists
and keep asking everyone why

INSPIRATION

I have brought you to this Greek village
famed for its honey
as others are for their bread or wine
Love-making kept us awake
half the night
afterwards the jiggers took over
and would not let us sleep
Cocks and crowing women
woke us from our troubled doze
We compared laughingly the red bruises
on our arms and cheeks
Your good mouth, as it always does,
made me drool
and my spirit rose at once
In this stupid century
addlepated professors and mechanics
decry Inspiration
Alas, their arms have never held her;
gazing at you, woman,
in this shy early morning light I could more easily
doubt the feel of the bare boards under my feet
Truly this goddess has being
—in you, in some rare almost forgotten poems
and the mountainous hills and sea
which are waiting for us to look at them,
this vinestem curling on our windowsill
this bee
Come, let us show them
the fierce lumps on our divine foreheads

Skyros, Greece
June 10, 1972

PARTY AT HYDRA
For Marianne

The white cormorants shaped like houses stare down at you.
A Greek Chagall perched them there on the crooked terraces.
The steep ascent is through a labyrinth of narrow streets
Cobbled with huge stones that speak only Arvanitika.
A surfeit of wisdom has made the stars above you eternally silent.
Many are ambushed by the silence and many never find their way
To the house where the perpetual party is going on.
If you are on the lookout for monsters or demons
You will not find their legs sprawled out in the terraces.
They are all assembled at the house threshing one another
With extracts from diaries whose pages fly open releasing beetles
That crawl along the grapevines and disappear into a night of ears.
Though only one head can be seen, several monsters have seven
And some have three and some no more than two. Beware of the one
Headed monster with an aspirin in his hand who'll devour you instead.
You know the number of heads each has by the small sucking winds
They make as they dissolve the salads and meats on their plates. So
Listen carefully holding a lighted incense stick for a talisman.
A rutting woman lets her smile float on your glass of punch.
You scoop it up to hand back to her on a soaked slice of lemonpeel.
A poet announces to everyone not listening he has begun a new poem.
He hears a spider growling at him from a suntanned cleavage
And at once pierces it with a metaphor using its blood for glue.
A married man discourses tenderly on love and poultices.
It is almost dark when a goddess appears beside you.
She guides your hand under her white robe and murmurs
'The sweat of invalids in medicine bottles is not love
And wisdom is love that has lost one of its testicles.
Desire is love's lubricant yet love is no wheel spinning in a groove.
Love resides neither in the body nor in the soul
But is a volatile element reconciling spirit to flesh.
Love is the holy seal of their interpenetration and unity
When they come together in the perfect moment of fusion.
If you wish to know more about love listen to the crickets on the moon
And emulate the silent shining of the stars but do not become one.'
When she vanishes your hand is a river you swim in forever.

THE ANTIPODEANS

I lived with a barren poet a day
And showed him poems who had none to show,
Crediting that sweet remark of Plato
That two souls are fused by love of beauty.
Yet what I saw was not love but envy
And what I heard were jeers like broken cries
Each time I moved him with a fine surprise
To make a deaf man hear, a blind one see.
I was amazed to find him so transformed;
Where was the joy that beauty should call out?
Why by an ideal love was he deformed
And all his kindly feelings put to rout?
Alas, men are so imperfectly made
They must curse the light that puts them into shade.

THE BENEDICTION

The Sabbath candles
my mother blesses
burn brightly

The flames dance
like little old men,
their visages
crumpled up with joy

To what music?
Or is it the silence
my mother
            has just shut the door on?

Souls are the candleflames'
blue centre
burning stilly;
I gaze entranced
at those of long departed
rabbinical ancestors
lecherous great-uncles
murdered kin
famed disputants in seminaries

Their shadows
linked as one
flicker
on the Friday-white tablecloth

While all the little old men
dance joyfully
in their orbits

SAVIOUR

The whole world was coming apart
   Mountains and valleys
Were changing places as if they were billows
   In a boiling ocean
But no shoreline or beach was to be seen
   To contain them
   Cities and plains
Having picked up and gone elsewhere
   Then day and night
Pulled away into two separate regions
   One wholly light, one wholly dark
   Being kept apart
By a single beach pebble.
   I was about
To dislodge it from its place
To allow light and dark to embrace
   For the sun I saw
Was beginning to move to another galaxy
   When a prophet
   Covered with hair
And wearing only a yellow straw hat
Stood up in the marketplace,
   A dazzling nail in his hand,
And pointed his plaited white beard
To a suppurating hole in the air.
   O mounting a chair
   Taller than Mount Vesuvius
   And standing there
He called to the frightened populace
   Let but an old man
   Throw me a hammer
And I'll nail the world back to rights again.
   But I saw no one stir
   And dead he fell at my feet
And it was I—I alone—who afterwards with a blue stone
   Plugged the hole in the air.

EARLY MORNING IN MITHYMNA

It is early morning in Mithymna

The sea has rolled itself back into place
and is patiently waiting to be looked at
by all the terraces

Roosters vie with one another
for sole possession of the sky
while their hens pick up the worms
shaken from it,
doing a dance
that just misses elegance by a feather

Every bird I see
carries in its beak
my love for the world

Not only for the gracious things in it
but for the ugly,
for vomit and dust
as for sunlight on a quiet empty pier
after the fishermen have gone home

I want to grab the waist
of the oldest hill
and dance with it
into the sea

To cover my face
with grass and leaves
and blow my ecstasy like green soap bubbles
into the air

The smell of honeysuckle unsettles me

I want to console all suicides

I want to climb the highest rooftop
in the village
and announce to all
that no one in it will ever die

I want to uproot all crosses
from the vaticans of the world,
all symbols of torture and death
from picture galleries, churches, museums
and the minds of men
where they have their dark beginnings

I want to open God's hands
to let fall on earth
the peace he keeps cupped in them
for everyone with joyous upturned face

ON SEEING AN OLD POET AND HIS WIFE

So all his passion has shrunk to this:
Three deathless poems and an old hag's kiss.

NO EXIT

The way his boy plucks them
off the Old Man's net
you'd think they were maybe scales
flakes of mica
or sequins
on a washed-up tulle dress

They're fish
—the tiniest I ever saw

And have just about stopped
squirming
          but for the obstinate few
still hanging on

Tell me
who's the Xenophon
of this Anabasis

Thalassa . . . Thalassa. . . .

They lift and flutter
like coloured bits of paper,
some all the way back to the sea
—if the wind falls that way

For the long-beaked birds
shaped astonishingly
like miniature flying coffins

THE COCKROACH

She was from Tokyo.
He was from Tabriz.
They met in a bookstore.
They both reached for the same book.
Excuse me, in Japanese.
Excuse me, in Persian.
The book was a treatise on the cockroach.
Each wanted the book.
There was only one copy.
They agreed to purchase it together.
Both were specialists in the make-up
and behaviour of cockroaches.
Fascinated lifelong students, they were.
Now they became fascinated with each other.
They fell in love looking at charts of cockroaches
ingesting whatever it is cockroaches ingest.
He took her to his apartment.
She took him to hers.
They went for long walks together.
They frequently talked about other things
besides cockroaches.
He read her his favourite Sanskrit poets.
She read him Haikus.
Examining the reproductive organs of their favourite
insect, their genitals became moist.
In his apartment; then in hers.
It was delightful.
It was romantic.
They were exceedingly happy.
The affair should have lasted forever.
It brought a shine to their eyes.
It did something to their voices.
They were very tender to each other.
He brought her some verses of his own.
She had a gift for him flown in from Tokyo.
Then one day they had a disagreement.
It was over the feeding habits of the cockroach.
He said one thing, she said another.

The disagreement became an argument.
The argument became a quarrel.
The quarrel became violent and bitter.
They could not agree on the feeding habits of the cockroach.
The gulf between them grew wider and wider.
He said this, she said that.
There could be no compromise.
Only one could be right.
They hissed at each other.
Their eyes filled with hatred.
They questioned each other's intelligence and lineage.
All the lovely, meaningful things they had said to each other
about cockroaches were forgotten.
It was sad.
It was very sad.
It ended with his taking his verses back.
She told him to keep the treatise on the cockroach
since plainly he needed it more than she did.
Bitch, in Persian.
Ignorant louse, in Japanese.
So the affair ended.
It was sad.
It was very sad.

THE BARONESS

He smiles gratefully when I tell him his beard
    makes him look like Solzhenitsyn
His wife is on some other island
    screwing other men
She will join him at the end of summer
There are so many, many islands in Greece
Her man-of-science hubby directs a Munich laboratory
    hopping in and out an enormous test-tube
Each morning he has his big erection in a glass cylinder
He'd rather stare at oxides than at a woman's breasts
    and the odourlessness of bismuth really turns him on
I've seen and felt his wife's breasts
They are not made of bismuth
    and, heated, give off a rank delicious smell
Erotic missionary, I see her bringing that smell
    to the remotest parts of the Aegean
Impregnating with it the flora of the countryside
Greece will never be the same when she's through
Even the colonels will be sent sprawling
    on their backs: I mean that literally
With her crushing their heads between her massive thighs
    or wiping her blonde twat with their tongues for napkins
What a woman! I call her the Baroness
She's not a woman, she's a phenomenon
    especially when she dances in a ruined castle
    with no one to applaud her performance but myself
A Valkyrie in a bikini!
What a sight! Yeats would have come in his velveteen pants
    a dozen times
And Eliot flushed his poems down the nearest toilet
O these sweet English boys talking about love and women
Take it from me, English poetry when it isn't the death wish
    is voyeurism and cuntsniffing
    but done with so much aplomb you take it
    for spirituality or a concern with art and the good life
If they were alive (were they ever?) and my Baroness
    laid a magical finger on them
    they'd both shit in their pants
    and run to their wives to clean them up

Or get a Harvard professor to do it for them
When my Baroness dances in a run-down medieval castle
    I think of her man-of-science hubby
    looking green and impotent
    away from his beloved molecules
And have wild, exhilarating thoughts
    about culture and civilization
    before I take her into my arms
And complete the dance with her under the broken turrets

SIGNS AND PORTENTS
For Eli Mandel

Ladies and gentlemen, all the important signs point to one thing:
    I am a fool
To begin with I got myself born into the wrong class and to the wrong
    parents
With my habits and inclinations I should have contrived to get myself
    dropped on a gold-threaded featherbed
And have selected for my father someone who was not a mystagogue
    but a munitions-maker
My mother was okay but she should have been my father
I've nothing against my brothers and sisters except that they were older
    and had more meat and muscle on their bones
It took me a long time to make out that my teachers were ball-less serfs
    in conspiracy with the Devil against intelligence and vitality
That when the strong spoke of law & order they meant legalized
    brigandage
That the weak speak of justice but mean revenge
That civilization is a pissoir with paintings by Rubens and Picasso
    on the walls: organ music by Handel and Bach
That not being handicapped in the least by vision or creativity, women
    are by far the stronger sex
That when they speak of love and romance they mean babies with hubby
    pinch-hitting for a baby rattle
That priests and rabbis have every good reason to believe in religion:
    it pays the rent
That poets are talented sickies to be avoided as one avoids
    the adder's bite
It took me too long to perceive that there is a God who doesn't exist
    anywhere, not in the heavens or in the hearts of men
That he reveals himself to the picked few only when he feels an
    uncontrollable desire to hear his own voice in the immense sol-
    itudes he has created for himself
And speaks to them only to comfort himself through the ineffable sound
    of his voice and to detect whether there has been any deterioration
    in its timbre through the centuries and ages
That I, Israel, can plainly hear his majestic vocables dripping
    from copse and corpse and the flash of a fish

Though I may never hope to make out what he is saying or why
    he prefers to say it the way he does
And that sunlight on leaves and water is his reassuring smile
It has taken me all these years to discover that everything except
    writing poems and making love ends up by finally boring me

THE TERRORIST

He has the face of a terrorist.
The other day I caught him reading Rilke.
He looks German too.
A German terrorist.
One of the Vanderfogels
with bombs in their canvas bags.
Hitler's legacy to the world.
His eyes are wolflike—cold and grey.
He smiles when we pass each other in the narrow street.
He asks me the time of day.
When I tell him he smiles and I observe his teeth:
white and strong like those of a wolf.
His lips are red, too red.
He sleeps on the beach.
His sleeping bag looks no different
from other sleeping bags.
He reads all the time, which is a bad sign.
He also sunbathes, stretched out in the only clean
alcove the beach owns.
He's also alone, which is another bad sign.
When I come to the beach he's already there
reading or sunbathing.
His presence irritates me.
His greeting irritates me.
His smile and grey eyes irritate me.
Also his white teeth, they irritate me too.
Our relationship can neither go forward nor retreat.
He has imposed an equilibrium I did not want.
It is that balance itself which has defined the distance
between us.
He wants to keep me to be smiled at all summer.
Maybe it makes him feel good to have someone like that.
Maybe he needs someone he can love;
not me, exactly, but someone.
Certain terrorists are like that.
Agh, but that's degenerate!
Loving someone and then machine-gunning hundreds of innocent
people, women with babes in their arms too.

I can see him doing it.
He looks the type.
Very quiet in a masterful way.
Then rat-a-tat, rat-a-tat, rat-a-tat
and the bleeding corpses are arrayed
around him like rose petals after a storm.
The coward.
Terrorists are cowards who kill for a cause:
for the poor, for Revolution, for the working-class.
If each poor man did his own killing
there would be no poor.
Someone like that I can respect.
He blows up a bank and the bank manager with it,
or a Trust with its President and five Vice-Presidents.
Poverty has ruined his life.
He has wanted joy.
He has wanted to straighten out his back.
He has wanted to be a human being.
His mind is filled with pictures of naked women
in alluring poses.
They take turns—two by two—massaging him.
They massage him everywhere.
Why should they do it only to bank managers and the presidents
of Trusts and Corporations?
He comes out of the favelas of Rio and blows them to hell.
Such a terrorist I can understand.
I would have him hanged or killed on the spot,
loathing anarchy more than injustice.
But I could respect and understand him.
But this one with the cold grey eyes who reads Rilke
and sunbathes by himself in the alcove.
—how can I respect him?
I wish he would go away and leave me the alcove.
I wish he would go away now.
I wish he would stop smiling at me.
I wish he would stop greeting me each time he sees me.
I hate him.
I hate him intensely.
I find myself wondering how I can be rid of him.
I find myself thinking obsessively about his imminent death.

A TALE WITH TEETH IN IT

The landlady is a fat Greek woman.
No, not fat, but stout, very stout.
Shaped like a pyramid, with head for apex.
She wears a black dress.
She speaks to me in fluent Greek
as it she'd known me all my life.
Is surprised and hurt
I don't understand a single word she's saying.
She begins again, slowly,
as with a child that is stupid.
Smiles frequently to indicate
she intends to be patient.
Ignorance and black superstition
have lined her face with attractive wrinkles.
She looks open-hearted but isn't.
(Greek landladies simply aren't.)
She looks open-minded but isn't that either.
(Open-minded? Are you kidding?)
Still there's something appealing
about her face and demeanour.
I put it down to an absence of toothache
and modern ideas.
Each time she smiles
I see the same yellowed stumps in her mouth
and the same black gaps between them.
Stumps and gaps never change places.
A pity. That way, I think, her smiles would be more intriguing.
Her mouth would have all the charm
of the unpredictable.
She startles me by shouting, "Stefano!"
Her husband appears as if from the ceiling.
He's shaped like a coffin, tapering
at both ends.
He's bald and has a faded red moustache.
He too addresses me
as if we'd grown up together,
fucked the same sheep on the hillside.
His wife looks on hopefully.

Her man will make the foreigner understand.
She has absolute confidence in him.
I smile helplessly.
Stefano smiles, showing fewer stumps and more gaps.
His wife smiles.
The three of us are standing in the room
I've come to rent.
We are all smiling.
Out of exasperation with me
man and wife begin talking to each other.
I notice they've stopped smiling.
That's only reasonable.
Stefano knows all his wife's gaps
and she knows his.
What's there to smile about?
Finally there's a breakthrough.
I write a figure on a piece of paper.
Stefano and the landlady
shake their heads delightedly as if astounded
the slow-witted foreigner can write.
Everyone is suddenly happy.
It's all been a question of money
from the start.
Drachmas, Sponduliks, Bread.
It's been settled and everyone is relieved.
We bare our teeth for a last smile.

XMAS EVE 1971, ZIHUATANEJO
For William Goodwin

Where were the men and where were the women robed in black
Where were the priests and nuns and the solemn processions
Now lights tear the jungle darkness, jukeboxes blare out their songs:
Packed in the open air cinema are all the reverent ones.

And only the lovely credulous children are in church
To hurrah His birthday and the marvelous manger story
Arrayed upon the altar; perhaps two or three old women
Crossing themselves in corners, remembering the Babe's past glory.

The children's eyes glisten as do those of the candy-stuffed
Animals that hang from the ceiling and lone and radiant star
But absent are prayer and song, the breathtaking enchantment:
For service a boy in frayed jeans casually sweeps the floor.

O sanguine fairytale, here replayed among pinatas
Long-beaked hungering birds, white hotels, the pullulating poor;
I too rejoice at the glad tidings: now none shall be maimed or killed
For this sweet handsome doll saves no one. Come, let us adore.

THE SILENCE

It grew from nothing
Inside me it grew
It grew in my veins and arteries
   In my bones and flesh
It mastered my blood
One day I found it curled up
   In my skull
Under my useless tongue
Now I have nothing to say
   To anyone

A WALK TO CHORA

From the road I'm walking on,
the crowded buildings of Chora
appear like a woven white shawl
laid across the throat of the mountain.

Fields are alive with insect noises;
under the bright mind-blowing sun
they're active communications centres,
the signals never dying down.

The crickets revolve their tunes
as if they're small hoops of sound
which they make and unmake
to scrape on the parched land

Olive trees and shrubbery too
are arrayed in their noise;
visible to listening eye and ear
seem their sharp metallic cries

And wearing their matted fells
sheep look judicial in this heat;
beside them the large sheep-dog
is out for good, dead-beat

While tethered to a forgotten tree
before she scratches her teat
a goat raising her hind leg
gives me a fascist salute

SNOWMAN

You are water and like water
slip through the fingers of my hand;
none can hold you, she said gaily,
none can hold you nor will I try.
But she froze me with her cold breath
and where she froze me there I stand.

TO MAOISTS

From my heart I rooted out Jehovah;
I spurned Moses and his Tables of Law
And tore up my father's phylacteries.
I did not turn from dragons to live with fleas.

THE TRANSFIGURATION

She's gross and smells unwashed
and has the face of a natural breeder,
one full of good-natured meaningless smiles,
her blue eyes clear as those of a mindless nun
from one of the villages of Quebec;
there's a ridiculousness about her gait
as though she were a self-moving piano
pushing ahead, now one castored end now the other.
Why then when I saw her clumsying
down the narrow pathway that leads to the sea
in the warm gloom of twilight and could make out
only the grey outline of her stolid shape
why did I have a sudden vision
of her entering a mysterious transfiguring grotto
where, if I followed, a laughing slender goddess
would embrace me and it would be she?

FOR AULD LANG SYNE
For Saul Berman

When my old schoolfellow
from Baron Byng
went into the insurance game
naturally I let him sell me
an insurance policy

Afterwards it was the furniture
business
and he persuaded me
I shouldn't live another hour
without an armchair
made from the finest imitation leather

Opening a men's haberdashery
for awhile he had me
the best-dressed poet
in the world

Then switching to cars
of course he sold me
the most expensive Jaguar
on the lot

Last week when he bought into
a funeral parlor
I decided the time had come
to put an ocean between us

AD MAJOREM DEI GLORIAM

Yesterday they were merely
two fish in the sea
and were not even known
to each other; two
ordinary, indistinguishable
fish among thousands and thousands
of their kind.
Now their pink skeletons
are laid out neatly
on my plate, side by side
like two gallant friends
or twin brothers martyred
in a cause that has gone badly;
a link (two links?)
in the great Chain of Being
that together with oil-scorched skins
soiled napkins and portions
of squeezed lemon
(browns, whites, pale yellows
and pinks—let's not omit
the indispensable pink skeleton)
make an arresting Still Life
for distressed mortals
forever seeking means
to replenish the spirit
and for the Cosmic Mind
whose aesthetic distancing
now and for all time
is never less than perfect.

FOR MAX WHO SHOWED ME
HIS FIRST GOOD POEM

Don't expect to be kissed on your cheeks
Or your forehead. The stars won't applaud
Nor will the moon shine any brighter.
Nothing will have changed in the cosmos

But keep on writing though no one cares;
And treat reviewers with calm disdain
Unless they praise you to the skies.
When asked to write reviews yourself ask

What reviews Homer and Shakespeare wrote.
Nor join clubs nor any Poets' Leagues;
If invited make it your excuse
You're presently too much occupied

Researching the well-known club-joining
Proclivities of Marlowe and Blake.
For enjoyment read minor poets
But write only for the truly great

Whose assessment is the final one
Along with that of posterity
Though the two, my son, are really one.
Seek Dante's praise, not John Colombo's

Never run after fame but let it
Come to you. Fame is to a poet
What a fair face is to a woman:
A great toner-up of the system

Giving its possessor joy and grace.
Nor hanker for money either, son;
Fortunately there's none to be had.
Therefore farther off is corruption

Anything with a moneytaint stinks;
Burn that into your soul. Ignoble
Lives that lost man who makes gold his aim.
I fathered you for holier ends

To live with greatness from day to day,
Avoiding the common joyless ruck;
Your emblem the proud scanning eagle
Alone under the pitiless sky

Be gentle and have a loving heart.
Then kick your dear father in the balls
And go your own sweet way to renown,
Knowing you're one of the lucky ones

MEMO TO A SUICIDE

When I was mad
about her
I bought all her daubs
—money on the barrel:
she wouldn't have it
any other way—
took her to expensive restaurants
movies and plays
lit up her body
with flowers and jewels
and with the fever
of an aging lover
threw in a summer's idyll
on the Riviera

You, Luke, hanged yourself
so that she could see
your blue tongue
sticking out at her
when she found you

from *The Pole Vaulter*

DEPARTED

I walk the streets
of Amsterdam
                    looking
everywhere for the faces
Rembrandt painted

The visages of burghers
unruffed & unruffled
(though a suspicion
in the clear light eyes
                    the world's not always
ordered for the best)
arise to confront me

Unchanged
as the weatherstained gables
in their chartered banks
in their sleek pleasure boats

But where
are gone the grizzled ecstatic
faces
          of the vehement crazy men
who dreamed and prayed?

THE SHADOW

I am a shadow. Everywhere, in the house
where I slip from my wife's embrace
as if her daily kiss turns me
inexplicably into vapour or a black cloud,
at the university where I teach teenagers
how to hide their emptiness and grow richer
than corn factors during a famine; even
my youngest son whom I love best
for he's my own childhood raised from
a cemetery of lies and guilts
cannot keep the awful metamorphosis
from happening or my uncontrollable
spastic feet from the trapdoor that sends me
swinging into space over the loneliest wolves

I release my shadow like a switchblade
or the cavernous grin of a ghost
as it spreads across the polished bannister
in failing traces that punctuate and pass,
even here in this well-lighted
Viennese hofbrau bursting with bodies
in clotted happy families of three or four
poised to reactivate bowel movements
through *brauten* and *schweinerfleisch*, to grease
with assorted dainties the secretions
of gland and skinpore; or playing cards
and drinking beer making a racket to awaken
Stahrenberg or that runt Dolfuss from the dead

I sit at my table, *nein* excuse me,
lie flat against the wall and manipulate
my filled glass like an aging acrobat
taking care not to spill a single drop
on their mothballed Nazi uniforms
or the undistinguished guttural faces
of the wives blanched by too much Catholic
piety—or is it pastry? Who wants to be

censorious at a moment like this, a moralist
when all are good-naturedly enjoying
the warm summery evening without a care,
stuffing their grudges against the world
a whole lifetime of self-hatred and resentment
into the tumblers they clink with friends
or in happy encircling arc with their neighbours?

Take me off the wall I shout from the wall,
don't leave me stretched out like some African skin
in a museum after the lights are extinguished
or like the silent spear in a corner absurd
and powerless menacing the ceiling;
teach me your indifference to great events
your boisterous pinkfaced affability as you slam
down your cards on the table as if they were fists
on an old Jew's skull, let me revel
in your ordinariness, in your guiltless murders
and the inescapable doom of your mediocrity
as you waltz down the Taborstrasse
with the Strausses, *vater und sohn*, directing
the orchestra with the baton of a clipped moustache

Teach me, O wretched modern clods
with lies and carnage in your genitalia,
how to love you, how to love every creature
on whom my shadow falls, humbled by the appalling
necessity that placed you here so that galaxies
may be explored and a divine few finally
defile through a ravine suspended only
by sunlight and music. Let me hug
you all to my breast, your mouths slavering
with goodwill and sincerity, my own no less
white and damp, I shout, but who hears my cries?
No one, no one. A tall man dressed for a fashionable
funeral at the Opera House rises invisibly
from one of the tables and gliding towards the door
scrapes off my shadow with his blue fingernails:
at dawn I grope my way to my child's hand

THE FINAL SOLUTION

It's been all cleared away, not a trace:
laughter keeps the ghosts in the cold ovens
and who can hear the whimpering of small children
or of beaten men and women, the hovering echoes,
when the nickelodeons play all day the latest Berliner
love ballads, not too loudly, just right?
Taste the blood in the perfect Rhenish wine
or smell the odour of fear when such lovely
well-scented frauleins are fiddling with the knobs
and smiling at the open-faced soldier in the corner?

History was having one of its fits—so what?
What does one do with a mad dog? One shoots it
finally and returns armless and bemedalled
to wife and children or goes to a Chaplin film
where in the accommodating dark the girlfriend
unzips your fly to warm her hands on your scrotum.
Heroes and villains, goodies and baddies, what
will you have to drink with your goulash? In art museums
together they're shown the mad beast wagging its tail
at a double-hooked nose that dissolves into ash

And appraised by gentlemen with clean fingernails
who admire a well-executed composition or pointed to
in hushed tones so that nothing of the novel frisson
be lost. Europe blew out its brains
for that frisson: gone forever are the poets and actors
the audacious comics that made Vienna and Warsaw
hold their sides with laughter. Gone, gone forever.
They will never return, these wild extravagant souls:
mediocrity stopped up their witty mouths,
envy salted the ground with their own sweet blood

Sealed up their light in the lightless halls of death.
Alas, the world cannot endure too much poetry:
a single cracked syllable—with a cognac—suffices.
I have seen the children of *reingemacht* Europe, their
queer incurious dead eyes and handsome blank faces,
leather straps and long matted hair their sole madness.
They have no need of wit or extravagance, they have
their knapsacks, their colourful all-purpose knapsacks.
The nickelodeon grinds on like fate, six fatties play cards:
the day is too ordinary for ghosts or griefs

MIDSUMMER'S DREAM IN THE VIENNA STADPARK

Auschwitz, as we know, is on the moon
And Belsen on Mars or Venus.
How can I not believe it?
The waltz strains are so entrancing

Anne Frank is alive and well
And so's her sister Margot;
In fact they're right here in the park
Seated beside the gentleman in the third row.

How handsome the two sisters look
—Anne's eyes, as always, are radiant;
They are drinking in the music
And can scarcely keep their feet from dancing.

And they praise the statue of Johann Strauss,
A single curve of pure delight;
Time sleeps on his violin
And he smiles at them all through the night.

Someone has gone to find their father;
He should be here any minute now.
Ah, happy man, run fast, faster.
Do not stop to wipe your brow.

For all in the park recognize Anne
And stand up as one to applaud her
Because though doomed herself she wept
When she saw gypsy children led to the gas chamber.

THE VENTRILOQUIST

The brightly painted puppets
are in their places again:

Smiling to one another
over the butchered meat of cows and sheep
the spiced legs and wings of braised chicken
talking chortling crowing
blinking their eyes in affection
or good humour, cracking jokes
and giving each other sly digs
to put the table in an uproar of merriment

To add to the realism
the pink-faced waiters are perspiring
the manager wearing frown and black gaberdine
hurries towards the solitary diner
and the radio plays a Mendelssohn *lied*

In a far corner of the restaurant
two shadowy figures at set intervals
move the Gothic chess pieces across a board
as if they were miniature landmines

And at a given signal
the six card-players stop their game
to argue hotly the political news of the day:
the brutal killing of a party leader
of surprising astuteness
and manoeuvrability

Unexpectedly I overhear from another table
someone say I adore you Lisl, I love you Lisl
and a puppet in slacks and purple blouse
murmur sadly I love you too Heinrich

Though I look everywhere for him
the diabolical ventriloquist
is nowhere to be seen

Vienna,
July 1973

109

FOR THE FRAULEIN FROM HAMBURG

Poor mortal
you show a white-coated tongue
to the world

Bone-weary of the political leaflet
hash
and the occasional excitation
of your clitoris

Even the misery
of other despoiled humans
superfluous like yourself
no longer cheers
or relieves the ache
of your cureless insignificance

You hold up fists
to be manacled, fraulein,
and shrewder decadents than you
will again congeal your nullity
into the slavemaster's whip

REQUIEM FOR A.M. KLEIN

I remember your cigarette-stained fingers
The rimless glasses that glinted with your wit
And the bowtie protruding
Under your chin like a spotted tongue

Your scholar's mind neat as your hair
And the jaunty self-loving complacencies
That made me think of plump pumpkin seeds
Falling from your mouth, the epigrams

I finally gave up counting
Scattering like the pigeons on St. Mark's square
When a piston ring suddenly explodes.
I still wonder at your psychological obtuseness

And the sentimentality each clever Jew
Misconstrues for sensitivity:
Fool's gold which you, O alchemist,
Changed into precious metal, solid and true

Warm-hearted egotist, my dear unforgettable Abe,
You were a medieval troubadour
Who somehow wandered into a lawyer's office
And could not find your way back again

Though the reverent adolescent
Like the Virgil which fee-less you taught him
Would have taken your hand and led you out
Muttering the learned hexameters like a charm

Now grey-haired I diet, quarrel with my son,
Watch a young girl make love to herself
Occasionally speak to God and for your sake
Resolve to listen without irony to young poets

But still muse on your bronzed tits of Justice.
Yes, here where every island has its immortal bard
I think of you with grateful tears and affection
And give them your fresh imperishable name

LILLIAN ROXON

Asthmatic and always stuffing your face;
Your lymph glands brimming with chemicals to control
Unavailingly your adiposity and sinister wheezings;
The sudden breathlessness that threatened each time
To unhook your fat body from your soul. . . .

You've taken the whole works into the grave
With you. After all the noisy convulsive shakes
Like those of a resistless locomotive rumbling
Out of the station—silence. Uncanny silence.
Not a single wheeze can ever startle you awake.

Death, the fathead, struck you when you were alone;
Stabbed that great heart of yours, sparing
The mediocrities and prudent losers your scorned.
So many lumps to choose from, their numbers increasing,
And that dull jerk must come and strike you down.

My dear incomparable Lilli, I find it strange to think
I shall never hear again your indecorous wit
Or see your wide luminous eyes glitter with humour
And affection. Unencumbered, now lighter than air
My fat companionable pole-vaulter, you leave the ground and soar.

TO THE WOMAN WITH THE SPEAKING EYES
For Rae Sampson

It is not men you fear
but the tenderness they make you feel for them

And your resentment is not against men
but against the unfair division of the universe
into pestle and mortar, mountain peaks and valleys

Dark your beautiful eyes and tragic:
they have seen too many fearsome transformations
of smooth pluckable mushrooms into clubs and truncheons

Your desirable breasts are a burden to you
and though your Caesarean cicatrice
is an arrow that points directly
to where all men and angels would wish to lie
your supple pleasure-promising legs are closed
against them like inhospitable Abrahams

Unsure of the planets that rule, finally
you walk away hand-in-hand with your pride
leaving behind your modern confusion
for philosophers to unravel

TERRORISTS

Insulted, forsaken exiles
harried, harrassed, shat on
learing
        Justice is heard only
when it speaks through the mouth
of a cannon

leaning
        Right lies waiting
to fly out of a gun barrel

learning weakness is the one crime
history never pardons or condones

Uselessly you bruise yourselves, squirming
against civilization's whipping post;
Black September wolfcubs
terrify only themselves

The Jewish terrorists, ah:
Maimonides, Spinoza, Freud,
Marx

The whole world is still quaking

FOR ANDREI AMALRIK

Who speaks up for you, Andrei Amalrik?
Worse yet, today for whom do you speak?
Forsaken and more alone than any heretic
Who whitened into ash—where are your guns? Your bombs?
Brave soul, you have none. You have none.

Into the gas ovens with you like a helpless Jew
Into the slave camps or Kolymna mines
You have a mind; it is your ruin
Imagination and spirit; they are your undoing
Integrity. Luckless man, in these times? You are doomed.

Your ears were not fashioned for loudspeakers
Your eyes for the blueprints of beehive utopias
Your published wit as packing for Lenin's ravings
The experts east and west want to squeeze oil
From your pores to keep their factory cylinders purring.

Your martyrdom means nothing to the young
With close-cropped slogans between their ears
And their terrible blank faces. Nothing. In East Berlin
To the red refuse swept up from every land
A thing to sneer at and entomb in Siberian silence.

You are a bitter portent for mankind, Andrei
As ominous as the death of Anne Frank
Swiftly the sun sinks and shadows mount the hill
Who besides yourself cares about freedom?
Only the wolves you see from your barred window.

POET'S BUST

Firmly he held the sword in his hand:
he glared at the snakecurled head in the mirror
and lopped it off with one sweep;
his senses extra sharp to the end,
he heard it fall at his feet

Untangled are the pendant curls,
lordly now is the smile on his lips;
his face inscrutably serene
melts the conqueror's heart of stone:
young girls gaze at the scaleless eyes and dream

POSTCARD
For Aviva

In Venice
when it stormed
(ah, where have the years fled?)
you clasped me to you
in terror and love

Each thunderclap
was a fresh embrace
under the sheets;
we were never so close
as when the elements
seemed bent to destroy us

Tonight
as if another
War of Liberation
were in progress
thunderclashes
rock Budapest
and flares
light up the city
to direct fiery
salvos of rain
against roofs and bridges

Marauders
are hammering
on the windowpanes
and I cower
under my blanket
—but where are you, my love?

WHAT I TOLD THE GHOST OF HAROLD LASKI

There are days when I think of nothing
but politics:
wasted precious hours taken
from poem-making love-making and fine conversations
about fellatio in ancient Abyssinia
or collecting and watering beach pebbles
to surface their magnificent colours
from somewhere deep inside them;
I've seen them brighten with a luminosity
no one in his right mind or not forced to
would ever impute to the faces of Franco
Richard Nixon or old sourpuss himself, Kosygin,
his lower bowel constipated with bolshevism

Name me three statesmen
who ever wrote a line of memorable poetry
I don't mean rhetoric, I mean poetry
though Lincoln's melancholia comes sometimes close
and the passion of Fox and Demosthenes

But would you really quote Lester Pearson
to the girlfriend taking off her panties
and you wanted the clinching line
to make it hot and good?
Or Dief the Chief though that adman's tag
rhymes with grief
at the funeral of a young much-loved child?

After all poetry is as private as a sigh
though the whole world hear it;
politics, public and impersonal
as a civic lavatory or bus:
it's the trough
at which all push and shove
the rich bastards that have too much
and the poor bastards that don't have enough

One day when I'm not expecting it to happen
I shall look up and see the Parliament buildings
all going up in pamphlets and smoke,
and seeking out the Prime Minister
I'll find him under his desk
haranguing a visiting contingent of pygmies
on the grace and benefits of lowliness.

Out of gratitude for his eloquence
they ask me to present him with a toupee
made from their daughters' pubic hair
before I wrap myself in the Maple Leaf
and make myself completely invisible.
Instead, I hand him this poem
and tell him to use it as a visa
for heaven

Yes, there are days when I think of nothing
but politics
but they are not my best days

MARRIAGE

The lover of the treacherous wife
dribbled poison into the king's ear

In no time the fair regal body
that had known only perfumes and oils

Blossomed with hideous pustules;
boils covered it from crown to toe

Ugly under the sun, the sleeping king
gave up his ghost to the battlements

One dark night a poet saw the powerless shade
and gave to it an immortal voice

PEACOCK

Moving slow and gorgeous
as in the feathered radiance
of a dream
and without defence
as Beauty and Delight
always have been,
he's the poet among birds

Only in a cage
where he can strut and astound
is he secure
from claws and fangs
indifferent
to the elegant loveliness
of his elongated vulnerable tail

Pride-besotted creature
to have so many eyes
and to be so blind

SOME OTHER DAY

In the morning I smoked my cigarette
had a cup of black coffee
and carefully went over my plan
for the destruction of the world

At night I rejoiced
alone in my room
at having put aside my scheme
to annihilate the world and all its inhabitants,
discovering once again
that great events roar over mankind
like the sea over the inert
stones and pebbles on the beach
and hearing the Greek fruit peddlers
shout through the narrow streets of Mithymna:
'Orea pragmata! Orea pragmata!
Beautiful things. I have beautiful things to sell.'

But it was the black kitten
I saw rolled up in the sunshine
like a tiny ball of fur
that stopped my thoughts like a period

THE BLACK QUEEN

Having the face of a worldlywise Greek cat
he tells me how one late afternoon
he was sleeping on the white sand
with a scorpion only inches from his head
readying its black stub
                     when his wife
who saw the menace from where she stood
awakened him with a harsh whisper
so this thing of death would not strike
from shock or sudden fear
                    and as if
the innocent shingle were a launching pad
he sprang up from his rosy dreams of life
and with a stone roiled the foul blackness
into the sand like the devil's instep

I tell him how I once swam solitary
through a minefield of jellyfish
and got myself stung in the eye
                    I saw
huge blue and yellow stars light up the water
and dance till they disappeared among the ferns
but the bright blister on my face was a reflex
I saw the green world through for weeks afterwards
and the mist
               on either side of the wide horizon

After that we played cards
and I pulled a straight flush
                   queen spade high

MITHYMNA CEMETERY

The villagers use it merely to pull off the flesh
from the skeleton,
then they come for the bones if they're not bones themselves
and bury them in the back yard

This busy traffic has gone on for centuries:
year in year out
corpses in skeletons out,
the bones cleaner
than the wings of that butterfly
hovering over my feet

The whitewashed walls are almost as tall as the cypresses
to keep the dead from clambering over them;
when the aging sexton closes the gate
you know they are all locked in securely for the night

Behind it the blue waters wrinkle and spume

The barren treeless hills
have not changed their places in aeons

Alcaeus and Sappho
may have sat on the selfsame stone
I am sitting on now
and looked out at them and at the sea

I should like to think so
it makes death's victory somehow less complete

MOLIBOS CAT

Her eyes are round with suspicion.
At your approach she runs away.
Children and grown-ups are her enemy,
not dogs which she can lick in a fair fight

Dogs don't suddenly kick a pregnant cat
for no reason at all
or blind her with a pointed stick.
No dog ever poured naphthalene on her fur
and afterwards put a lighted match to her tail.
No dog ever wanted to hobble her for life
by sawing off one of her front paws

She has been around humans for a long time
and knows their true nature
—knows it better than Blaise Pascal
who flopped down on his knees and prayed.
Look at her curled up on the ledge;
even in sleep her long face is reserved and melancholy.

One can imagine Heraclitos, the weeping philosopher,
looking like that

THE IDEAL AMONG VACATIONISTS

I pick myself up from the beach
to leave my impress on the stones and pebbles

Visible to no one else but me,
it is intact and infrangible as a concept

It is also more permanent than caves or mountains:
not even the tide can haul it into the sea

Each time I look for it, is is plainly there
like Honoré de Balzac's covert masterpiece

Sunbathers trip over it, mistakenly thinking
it is a stone bigger and more jagged than the rest

Who knows how many other outlines lie beside it
and whether Eternity has made them restless

Like them it too is cold to middle-class Athenians
whose churning mouths spit out clichés and *tzatziki*

However fiery, the sun cannot use my figure
to fry the oils and creams dripping from their bodies

It is indifferent to dowries and gold watches
for in the dark the constellations keep guard over it

When I return early next morning
I shall see my ideal shape sprouting between the stones

PROTEUS AND NYMPH
For Molly

I put down my book
    and stare at the distant haze;
the loud-voiced Greeks around me
    chomping on their fish and *peponi*
must reckon I'm having age-old thoughts
    on the human condition.
Noisy fools. I'm thinking of the waves
    gently cupping the breasts
of the lovely nymph just risen from the sea
    and the water lapping
her thighs and her delicate love-cleft

When she swims away
    she pulls my thoughts after her
in watery streaks of light. I become
    the sea around her
and she nestles in my long green arms
    or is held in the flowing
wavelets of my white hair. I billow
    above her like a dolphin
stroke her limbs and nip her rosy neck and shoulders
    with sharp unceasing kisses
till languorously she slips to the ribbed sand
    where under the haloing starfish
fern weed and enamoured seasnake I quiver
    between her silver thighs

GREEK FLY

Wings filled with divine inner chaos

Bringing bazouki music to chairs, walls, tables
and the long thin ouzo glasses on the table
or taking its inspired frenzies up to the ceiling,
spotted picture frames and oleographs
or to the taciturn wife and husband whose day
begins with their disappointment in each other

Rubbing the golden moments between its legs
the rapturous fly comes to rest on a nail
making it buzz with the unceasing malice
of an old woman's tongue: the kitchen
is loud with its dry bright-hued gossip and abuse;
then landing on my shoulder the fly announces
to saucepans, forks, still uneaten eggs
and to all the crumbs the splendid news
that my poems like my vaccinated arm
are good for all borders

Shifting to another fleshly promontory
it stands on one leg like a proud Talmudic scholar
and recites the entire Odyssey
and is about to begin the Iliad
when catching sight of itself in the mirror
it leaps into the air like Nureyev
and gives a breath-taking performance
of a fly chasing itself until it's caught

The fly brings ripe hayfields into the room
the smell of cows and summer barnyards
the innocence of children clapping their hands in play
Mao and the Chinese revolution that sent it here
and all the poems ever written about mortality
and Emily dying to its ever fainter buzz;
head between its legs it thinks hard about life's brevity
then like a mad Euripidean Greek it drops
a billion eggs to fertilize its unkillable tragic splendour

It takes chances, this fly, like a poet;
it threads the air under the wife's frown
and recklessly settles on her puckered forehead
as if it were the face of Papadopoulos lying in his coffin
then shamelessly cleans its legs before her eyes
when her loathing for her husband in her open palm
descends on it with all the unerring ferocity
of repressed lasciviousness and thirteen years
of successful marriage

There it lies on the floor
waiting for the funeral orations to begin

Molibos, Lesbos,
August 6, 1973

GANYMEDE

Sitting in a taverna
among garrulous life-loving Greeks,
the morning sunshine
falling on tables and glasses,
I am suddenly pierced
by a Jove-sent arrow
of unreasonable joy

It was Ganymede
who nipped me with it,
a smiling rogue of six
gathering the bottletops
lying on the floor
like fallen miniature crowns
and emptying
their small bowls of sunlight
into his pockets

I greet him
with a secret sign
and my old eyes
are as gay as his

CH'AN ARTIST

Through the loving contemplation
of transiency and mutability
I received a foretaste of eternity
and saw with luminous certitude
that the wheel turned and did not turn

Drawing a roseleaf for ten years
I flowed at last into the leaf;
I shuddered at the raindrop's touch
till I became raindrop and splash:
now I draw the roseleaf perfectly

THE COASTAL MIND

On the electric train
that's taking me to Gosford
what I think of
                    as it rounds
the long solitary beaches and lagoons
is how Wagner
                    would be out of place here
too melodramatic too noisty too showing off
Bach, yes, maybe Sibelius or Mahler
Mendelssohn and Bizet definitely not
                                        Yet
ultimately this country will make
its own music
                    uneuropean
as its marsupials
and like them wary
of softer more tender responses

From
       the rattling little train
separating me from the sunshine and gloom
of Sydney the beerdrinking nihilists
who meet each Friday at the same pub
houses sheds petrol stations bridges
drop into the dry white mouth of space
forever open to gulp
                   and excrete them
unchewed yet crumbling visibly
at the foot
of the impenetrable bush

                 Everything human
in this huge dead continent is pushed
to that green periphery: the painted gates cars
children tools and red bulldozers
I see with turned head
           now leaking softly
into the diminishing distance
even the coastal mind running after them
that contemplates   holds on   finally lets go

AUSTRALIAN BUSH

I am about to get lost
in the Austrailian bush

Behind me
dusty and obscure
stretches the road convicts
laid down
           their lives for;
in front of the ghostly gumtrees
drop their skins
like snakes

The bush is a wily old grandmother
that never had children,
forever wiping the grey-green ichor
streaming from her eyes

Birdcries are lost in her hair
and become one more smudge

I am startled
by the dry silence
into which my flesh sinks
as if I were a swaddled whisper,
by the low-breathing absence
that takes me quietly in

All the brown dead leaves
strewn along the road
keep telling me
           there's no death,
the black wounds and sores
of dateless trunks
           mouth my resurrection

Why then does the knowing
not refresh or gladden

Why instead
do I sit down at the sanded rim
feeling suddenly burdened and weary
as if the agonized trees
had lowered
                all their accumulated aeons
onto my fragile human back

POLE-VAULTER

Now that grey fluff
covers my chest
and it's the glasses on my nose
that sparkle, not my eyes
what the horny girls
                    want from me
is advice on
how to allure young men;
                                    those
with ideas in their head
and pimples on their ass,
my final opinion
on the Theaetetus

They say at my age
I should be guru or sage,
not foolishly behave
like passion's slave

Ignorant trulls
in a cold land;
age will dry their flesh
and wrinkle it with useless folds.
Spry and drugged with love
I pole-vault
                    over my grave

FUNERARIA 'OLEA'

In bold black letters:
SERVICIO DIA Y NOCHE
Obviously this is not a dead business.

It is a thriving business.
Go in,
See for yourselves the white coffins
Lying in wait for the townspeople.

The tiniest caskets
Are the most numerous;
The women in these parts
Are always pregnant with them.

Zihuatanejo, Mexico

EPIGRAM FOR A.M. KLEIN

They say you keep the devils laughing by your wit
And all the furnaces stilled that they may hear it.

BODHIDHARMA

From what sputtering taper
was my light kindled
. . . to sputter in its turn

Detached iotas of flame
fall into the Vast Emptiness
to turn up fragments of poems
floating on its nearest facet.
I roar with furious laughter.

My pleasure in discomfiting
enemies and friends alike
is a gift from the Gautama himself.

And where I turn
I meet myself
striding the other way.

At sudden moments
power can come flooding in
from unseen major stars, from geese
and leaping goats
to soak all my follicles
in the sweetness of Buddhi.

That's why my face
looks like a clenched fist
and I am always irascible.

YOUNG COUPLE AT LUM FONG HOTEL

When I see you
        smiling
at each other
and nakedly showing
the appetite in your hands and eyes

I forget the chattering old men
        with bladder trouble
and slack-bellied blear-eyed women
who moan
        over their hard nocturnal stools
as once with equal vehemence
they rocked and moaned
in the furious exertions of love

Each other's unbreaking pole
        of imagination and love
you vault over
        wisdom greying at the roots
and smelling of unalterable defeats,
the will-to-power that fleers
        out of skincreases and hemorrhoids

O my oblivious lovers
from my table
        I applaud silently
as you rise
with perfect grace and disdain

Penang,
December 7, 1973

from *Seventy-Five Greek Poems 1951-1974*

HELIOS

Behind the harbour houses, the trees,
Helios has dropped from sight;
he's taken his bright runner with him
woven from water and light

For the fishermen's eyes all day
it blazed, it sparkled and shone;
they turned to their nets one instant
and the emblazoned strip was gone

He travels around the world, the sun;
and in what other coves I wonder
does he unroll his carpet
for the lovely Thetis to walk on

BLACKOUT

Suddenly everyone feels
weightless as a whisper
                                unreal
and drained of substantiality;
most pitiful seem the children,
pointless as their own queries

The restaurant is lit
by tiny candleflares on each table;
the shadows flickering on the wall
could be Turks advancing or retreating,
Achilles' spear, the greaves of Ajax

The scene is as old as man's ferocity;
so is the scarcely concealed excitement
at the approach of catastrophe,
the prospect of something unusual
about to happen
                        to confer meaning
on lives otherwise meaningless
and without glory

O Habbakuk
slide down from your heavenly terebinth
convince us
                    huddled around this martial box
it is punishment for some sin
done out of anger or pride:
come, make our possible deaths
welcome and intelligible

This day
a hundred handsome young Greeks
a hundred handsome young Turks
had their blood spilled out
like so much slop

O JERUSALEM

Jerusalem, you will be betrayed again and again:
not by the brave young men who die for you
with military cries on their blue lips
—never by these
                    And never by the scholars
who know each sunken goat-track
that winds somehow into your legend, your great name
and not by those dreamers
                            who looking for the beginnings
of your strange wizardry ascend from storied darkness
holding dust and warped harps in their blistered hands

These will always find you and bring you
offerings of blood and bone
                            lowering their grave eyes
as to an idol made neither of wood nor stone
nor brick nor any metal
                    yet clearly visible
as through sitting on a jewelled throne
                                    O Jerusalem
you are too pure and break men's hearts
you are a dream of prophets, not for our clay,
and drive men mad by your promised
impossible peace, your harrowing oracles of love;
and how may we walk upon this earth
                    with forceful human stir
unless we betray you and adore?

A DREAM AT PANGRATI

without fail
the dynamitings begin at 7:45 a.m.
not letting me complete
my dream of you

each time
it is a different dream

one night
I stroke your uncovered thigh
another I kiss your navel

last week my head between your breasts
white and superb
I was Alexander
my legs spanning the Hellespont

but this morning's dream was the best:
without a stitch on
you flew into my embrace
crying wildly, "I am yours, yours only"

exactly at 7:45 a.m.
that dream was shattered too

THE CASTLE

They who built this castle
did they in its spacious courtyards dance
and did their fine ladies
display bejewelled hands?

Where are the fine ladies now
and where are their gallants?
All are gone, my love, all
grey dust under your heel

From this distant hill
the ruin looks like a trepanned skull
that mocks brides and fishermen
and even the stars and the sun

And you and all fine ladies
may see at any hour
the ironic scraping sand
dance in each crumbling tower

ITHACA

The tremulous moment he works and waits for
when the difficult poem is almost done
and only demands the fine transposition
of a single line, the smallest change in tone

Is the imperial moment just before
the relieving ambiguities of ejaculation,
when he can still urge on his ecstasy
and ecstasy and fate are one

Is Helios waiting in the blue sky for
the zenith's inevitable hammerstroke
timed to fall on his brass gong
at the exact instant of plenitude and decline

The total white exquisiteness before corruption
when the wave's wide flaunting crest
with smash and tumult prepares to break
into bleak nothingness on Ithaca's shore

REUNION AT THE HILTON

You walked into my room
bringing the misspent years with you

Like two grey-haired children at play
we re-arranged them

First on your lap
then on mine

HER MEDITERRANEAN MIND

Her Meditterranean mind
is like her cunt
—spongy

With the sponge
between her thighs
she wipes away
all distinctions

Her lascivious mouth
draws all men on,
finally down

There
there's no base or noble
exalted or low
all are laid low there
all lie equal there

O totalitarian state
and dearest country
giving to men
fraternity and equality
but not liberty

O humid slit
O welcoming grave
that buries his hopes and bones,
the hairy grass
curling over them
black as death

THE BEARD

This film critic from Los Angeles
plans to seduce him
                        with her knowledge
of contemporary flicks
and 18th century literature

Her well-lubricated body
glistens provocatively
                        under the hot sun
'She does everything with everybody'
is her reputation
among the Greek youths of the village

He sees a lipsticked vagina
forming syllables
                        on the pebbled beach
and black hairs beginning to sprout
all around her open mouth

TAKE IT ALL IN

Eyes, take it all in

Even that old Cretan soak you see
with the repulsive puffy lips
and blackened stumps of tooth

Even the vomit
at his feet

When I am dead
and the light is gone out of you
forever
you will not see this

You will see nothing

You will dissolve as noiselessly
into the moist earth
as these two lumps of sugar
in the glass of tea
I hold in my trembling hand

THE SHARK

In some quiet bay
or deserted inlet
he is waiting for me

It is noon
there is a stillness on water and land
as if some primal god is about to speak;
in the sky
not a single bird is to be seen flying

I shall swim out towards him
bringing him my incurable moral ache
and my cancered liver,
memories of women laughter Greek islands
griefs and humiliations I could find no words for

I want him to be black, wholly black
I want him to be famished and solitary
I want him to be quietly ready for me
as if he were the angel of death

The last thing I want my alive eyes
to behold before I close them forever
are his ripsaw teeth.

BYRON EXHIBITION AT THE BENAKI MUSEUM

In this quiet room my noble lord still roars
He hated all despots but he loved the whores

          *

Most graciously the colonels let us see
The sword of him who died to make Greece free

Athens
June 26, 1974

FLYTRAP

It is the agony of an expiring
Achilles or Lear
my son watches happening
on the white saucer
—his private Globe theatre

Or it's opera:
to the rising blare of its own wings
the stricken fly
storms and lurches
across the brightly prepared stage
like an outraged protesting
Rigoletto

"This one has had it," he says tenderly
when La Mouche rubs her delicate legs
to commence her frantic dance of death;
and feeling a surge of power
he broods over her ineluctable doom
as she goes into her last breath-taking spin

(O tragic joy
that softens eyes and mouth)

Hour after hour
my youngest son watches
the poor ignorant migs alighting
on the poisonous red square
and cannot have enough
of the subtlest elation
known to man

THE HELLENES

When the ancient enemy attacks,
islands and mainland freeze
into one solid phalanx
bristling with cannon and fierce moustaches;
there are no royalists and rightists
no left opposition
                    only Greeks eager to die
for the bitter lemons they will never squeeze
over their dogfish and *souvlaki*

They come down from their barren hills
they come out of their quiet valleys and ravines
smelling of olive oil, dung and sheep
they come out of their whitewashed homes
with slow dignity and resolve
manifest
            in the way they grip their muskets,
in their deliberate walk and talk

Even Pericles, the scrawny owner of the one
kafenion in the village,
plays only martial music in his nickelodeon;
even our asthmatic coffee-drinking grocer, Mr. Big,
now salutes sharply over each sale of *feta*;
even the grey-haired tailor sits up straightbacked
    as he threads his needle

Silent, their furrowed faces laned with tears,
the women watch them forming
into small dark clots
            on the dusty arterial roads

THE UNWAVERING EYE

Before my eyes
the green heads of drowned sailors
rise up and disappear at the water's edge;
the jagged stones on the beach
lie grey and menacing;
in the distance
the hills fold silently
into each other
to encircle the sea
like a Cyclops' hairy arm.

Above them, above ceaseless war,
the sun's glaucomic eye
journeys towards dissolution

Once, in a smiling bay
Nietzsche, hero and martyr,
beheld the gleaming spears
and shrieked, "Superman!"
He died innocent, a gentle lunatic

The abyss belched
and pulled him downward
by the two ends of his drooping moustache

Now I cannot look
at a solitary sunlit stone
and not think of Nietzsche's unwavering eye

INDEX OF TITLES

INDEX OF FIRST LINES